ARBITRARY BORDERS

Political Boundaries in World History

The Division of the Middle East
The Treaty of Sèvres

Northern Ireland and England
The Troubles

The Great Wall of China

The Green Line
The Division of Palestine

The Iron Curtain
The Cold War in Europe

The Mason–Dixon Line

Vietnam: The 17th Parallel

**Korea: The 38th Parallel and
the Demilitarized Zone**

The U.S.–Mexico Border
The Treaty of Guadalupe Hidalgo

ARBITRARY BORDERS

Political Boundaries in World History

Northern Ireland and England

The Troubles

Robert C. Cottrell

Foreword by
Senator George J. Mitchell

Introduction by
James I. Matray
California State University, Chico

CHELSEA HOUSE
P U B L I S H E R S
A Haights Cross Communications Company
Philadelphia

FRONTIS The island of Ireland (Eire) consists of the Republic of Ireland and, in the northeast, Northern Ireland which is an administrative unit of the United Kingdom.

CHELSEA HOUSE PUBLISHERS

VP, NEW PRODUCT DEVELOPMENT Sally Cheney
DIRECTOR OF PRODUCTION Kim Shinners
CREATIVE MANAGER Takeshi Takahashi
MANUFACTURING MANAGER Diann Grasse

Staff for NORTHERN IRELAND AND ENGLAND

EXECUTIVE EDITOR Lee Marcott
PRODUCTION EDITOR Noelle Nardone
PICTURE RESEARCHER 21st Century Publishing and Communications, Inc.
SERIES DESIGNER Keith Trego
COVER DESIGNER Keith Trego
LAYOUT EJB Publishing Services

A Haights Cross Communications Company

www.chelseahouse.com

First Printing

9 8 7 6 5 4 3 2 1

Library of Congress Cataloging-in-Publication Data

Cottrell, Robert C., 1950-
  Northern Ireland and England : the troubles / Robert C. Cottrell.
    p. cm. — (Arbitrary borders)
  Includes bibliographical references and index.
  ISBN 0-7910-8020-X
1. Northern Ireland—History. 2. Northern Ireland—Relations—England. 3.
England—Relations—Northern Ireland. 4. Political violence—Northern Ireland. 5.
Social conflict—Northern Ireland. 6. Irish unification question. I. Title. II. Series.
  DA990.U46C686 2004
  941.60824—dc22
                                  2004014440

Dedicated to Sue

Contents

Foreword

Senator George J. Mitchell

I spent years working for peace in Northern Ireland and in the Middle East. I also made many visits to the Balkans during the long and violent conflict there.

Each of the three areas is unique; so is each conflict. But there are also some similarities: in each, there are differences over religion, national identity, and territory.

Deep religious differences that lead to murderous hostility are common in human history. Competing aspirations involving national identity are more recent occurrences, but often have been just as deadly.

Territorial disputes—two or more people claiming the same land—are as old as humankind. Almost without exception, such disputes have been a factor in recent conflicts. It is impossible to calculate the extent to which the demand for land—as opposed to religion, national identity, or other factors—figures in the motivation of people caught up in conflict. In my experience it is a substantial factor that has played a role in each of the three conflicts mentioned above.

In Northern Ireland and the Middle East, the location of the border was a major factor in igniting and sustaining the conflict. And it is memorialized in a dramatic and visible way: through the construction of large walls whose purpose is to physically separate the two communities.

In Belfast, the capital and largest city in Northern Ireland, the so-called "Peace Line" cuts through the heart of the city, right across urban streets. Up to thirty feet high in places, topped with barbed wire in others, it is an ugly reminder of the duration and intensity of the conflict.

In the Middle East, as I write these words, the government of Israel has embarked on a huge and controversial effort to construct a security fence roughly along the line that separates Israel from the West Bank.

Having served a tour of duty with the U.S. Army in Berlin, which was once the site of the best known of modern walls, I am skeptical of their long-term value, although they often serve short-term needs. But it cannot be said that such structures represent a new idea. Ancient China built the Great Wall to deter nomadic Mongol tribes from attacking its population.

In much the same way, other early societies established boundaries and fortified them militarily to achieve the goal of self-protection. Borders always have separated people. Indeed, that is their purpose.

This series of books examines the important and timely issue of the significance of arbitrary borders in history. Each volume focuses attention on a territorial division, but the analytical approach is more comprehensive. These studies describe arbitrary borders as places where people interact differently from the way they would if the boundary did not exist. This pattern is especially pronounced where there is no geographic reason for the boundary and no history recognizing its legitimacy. Even though many borders have been defined without legal precision, governments frequently have provided vigorous monitoring and military defense for them.

This series will show how the migration of people and exchange of goods almost always work to undermine the separation that borders seek to maintain. The continuing evolution of a European community provides a contemporary example illustrating this point, most obviously with the adoption of a single currency. Moreover, even former Soviet bloc nations have eliminated barriers to economic and political integration.

Globalization has emerged as one of the most powerful forces in international affairs during the twenty-first century. Not only have markets for the exchange of goods and services become genuinely worldwide, but instant communication and sharing of information have shattered old barriers separating people. Some scholars even argue that globalization has made the entire concept of a territorial nation-state irrelevant. Although the assertion is certainly premature and probably wrong, it highlights the importance of recognizing how borders often have reflected and affirmed the cultural, ethnic, or linguistic perimeters that define a people or a country.

Since the Cold War ended, competition over resources or a variety of interests threaten boundaries more than ever, resulting in contentious interaction, conflict, adaptation, and intermixture. How people define their borders is also a factor in determining how events develop in the surrounding region. This series will provide detailed descriptions of selected arbitrary borders in history with the objective of providing insights on how artificial boundaries separating people will influence international affairs during the next century.

Senator George J. Mitchell
October 2003

Introduction

James I. Matray
California State University, Chico

Throughout history, borders have separated people. Scholars have devoted considerable attention to assessing the significance and impact of territorial boundaries on the course of human history, explaining how they often have been sources of controversy and conflict. In the modern age, the rise of nation-states in Europe created the need for governments to negotiate treaties to confirm boundary lines that periodically changed as a consequence of wars and revolutions. European expansion in the nineteenth century imposed new borders on Africa and Asia. Many native peoples viewed these boundaries as arbitrary and, after independence, continued to contest their legitimacy. At the end of both world wars in the twentieth century, world leaders drew artificial and impermanent lines separating assorted people around the globe. Borders certainly are among the most important factors that have influenced the development of world affairs.

Chelsea House Publishers decided to publish a collection of books looking at arbitrary borders in history in response to the revival of the nuclear crisis in North Korea in October 2002. Recent tensions on the Korean peninsula are a direct consequence of Korea's partition at the 38th parallel at the end of World War II. Other nations in human history have suffered because of similar artificial divisions that have been the result of either international or domestic factors and often a combination of both. In the case of Korea, the United States and the Soviet Union decided in August 1945 to divide the country into two zones of military occupation ostensibly to facilitate the surrender of Japanese forces. However, a political contest was then underway inside Korea to determine the future of the nation after forty years of Japanese colonial rule. The Cold War then created two Koreas with sharply contrasting political, social, and economic systems that symbolized an ideological split among the Korean people. Borders separate people, but rarely prevent their economic, political, social, and cultural interaction. But in Korea, an artificial border has existed since 1945 as a nearly impenetrable barrier precluding meaningful contact between two portions of the same population. Ultimately, two authentic Koreas emerged, exposing how an arbitrary boundary can create circumstances resulting even in the permanent division of a homogeneous people in a historically united land.

Korea's experience in dealing with artificial division may well be unique, but it is not without historical parallels. The first set of books in this series on arbitrary boundaries will provide description and analysis of the division of the Middle East after World War I, the Iron Curtain in Central Europe during the Cold War, the United States-Mexico border, the 17th parallel in Vietnam, and the Mason-Dixon Line. A second set of books will address the Great Wall in China, the Green Line in Israel, and the 38th parallel and demilitarized zone in Korea. Finally, there will be volumes describing how discord over artificial borders in the Louisiana Territory, Northern Ireland, and Czechoslovakia reflected fundamental disputes about sovereignty, religion, and ethnicity. Admittedly, there are many significant differences between these boundaries, but these books will strive to cover as many common themes as possible. In so doing, each will help readers conceptualize how complex factors such as colonialism, culture, and economics determine the nature of contact between people along these borders. Although globalization has emerged as a powerful force working against the creation and maintenance of lines separating people, boundaries likely will endure as factors having a persistent influence on world events. This series of books will provide insights about the impact of arbitrary borders on human history and how such borders continue to shape the modern world.

James I. Matray
Chico, California
April 2004

1

Bloody Sunday

On the cool, crisp morning of Sunday, January 30, 1972, crack British paratroopers (Paras) fired on Irish Catholic demonstrators in the community of Derry, located in the southwestern tip of strife-torn Northern Ireland. Less than half-an-hour passed before 30 men and 1 woman had been shot, with 13 suffering fatal wounds from the bullets, fired out of high-powered rifles, that slammed into their bodies. The already fractured state of Northern Ireland would never be the same after "Bloody Sunday," the name given to that fateful day, as tensions escalated markedly. Indeed, 1972 proved to be the deadliest year of the period of violence in Northern Ireland called the Troubles, as Catholics, Protestants, British soldiers, and British officials became ensnared in a cycle of seemingly ever-increasing violence. Meant to provide a lesson, Bloody Sunday instead helped to revitalize the Irish Republican Army (IRA), which in turn enabled Protestant paramilitary organizations to flourish.

Derry, ironically or appropriately enough, is situated on the near outermost corner of Northern Ireland, only a short distance from the border that separates it from the Irish Republic. During the early seventeenth century, as part of a deliberate effort to transform the ethnic and religious makeup of the Northern Counties, English officials brought new settlers, many of them Scottish Presbyterians, into Londonderry, where they confiscated the best land. These Protestant settlements were called plantations. Irish Catholics, along with most Protestant residents, referred to the developing community as Derry, which soon was ringed with great walls, constructed by English planters. The barriers, as journalists Peter Pringle and Philip Jacobson note, symbolized Protestant hegemony (dominance), and helped to stave off an assault by King James II of England, who was battling to regain his crown from a Dutch challenger, William of Orange. With the passage of time, residential areas—many of them Catholic—sprouted up beyond Derry's walls; the main Catholic district, only paling in comparison to its Protestant counterpart, was called the Bogside.

A British soldier drags a Catholic protester during the Bloody Sunday killings on Sunday, January 30, 1972. British paratroopers shot 1 woman and 12 men dead in Londonderry, Northern Ireland, in the span of about half an hour.

Following World War I, as nationalist sentiment surged forth, the British government agreed in 1921 to the establishment of the Irish Free State, featuring 26 Counties; among these were three in the north—Donegal, Cavan, and Monaghan—long part of the province of Ulster. Ulster's six remaining counties— Antrim, Armagh, Down, Derry, Fermanagh, and Tyrone—made up the state of Northern Ireland. The Anglo-Irish Treaty of December 1922 affirmed that the Irish Free State would become a British commonwealth (in 1949, the Irish Republic left the commonwealth). This cementing of partition proved unhappy for Ireland's Catholics, who continued to envision a unified Irish nation. Recognizing that their religious brethren were badly out- numbered in the South, Protestants delighted in the fact that they made up a majority of the population in the North.

As was true throughout Northern Ireland, the Catholic residents of Derry viewed themselves as discriminated against in terms of political representation, housing, and employment. Even with a Catholic majority, Derry was dominated politically by Protestants and *Unionists* (also called *Loyalists*), who insisted on Northern Ireland's remaining part of the United Kingdom. In 1954, the British Labour Party warned that high levels of unemployment could result in grave political difficulties in Derry and Newry. Eleven years later, a Unionist Member of Parliament (MP) exclaimed, "You cannot run away from ... Derry City where the population is 60 per cent Nationalist and 34 per cent Unionist. You cannot maintain Ulster this way."[1] Northern Ireland remained, as Jack Holland has indicated, a one-party state, something that was a rarity in Western Europe. This proved still more unsettling to Catholics, because political control often translated into control over the handing out of jobs and housing allocations. Derry's Bogside suffered unemployment of 20 to 30 percent, with corresponding social dislocations. The poet Seamus Deane was heard to say, "Bogside was once a street. Now it is a condition."[2] A Unionist MP warned, "If ever a community had a right to demonstrate against a denial of civil rights, Derry is the finest example."[3]

The sense of disfranchisement resulted in the development of a civil rights movement in Northern Ireland, which drew inspiration from the campaign by African-Americans conducted in the United States after World War II. To stave off the eviction of families from the Creggan, another district in Derry, activists employed direct action tactics, resisting the police. Several protest groups emerged, including the People's Action League and the Derry Unemployed Action Committee. For John Hume, a Northern Ireland politician and leading figure in the civil rights movement who believed that the Catholic-Protestant divide could be overcome, the non-violent tenets of Martin Luther King Jr. proved inspirational. Socialists, like many *nationalists* (those advocating the independence of Northern Ireland from Great Britain; also called *republicans*) had long reasoned that workers could surmount sectarianism, which the newly formed Northern Ireland Civil Rights Association (NICRA) hoped to avoid. Radicals, such as Eamonn McCann, who grew up in Derry's Bogside, joined the People's Democracy (a militant, student-dominated organization), urging both Catholics and Protestants to support revolution.

By 1968, the NICRA was conducting marches and sit-ins to garner attention for its demand that basic human rights be sustained and abuses of power curbed. Responding to a request by the Derry Housing Action Committee, the NICRA carried out one of its first marches in Derry on October 5, 1968. Most of the participants expressed concerns about jobs, housing, and equality of treatment, but some came determined to trigger a confrontation with authorities. Indeed, a few socialists sought "to provoke the police into overreaction," while the IRA also showed up. Both McCann and Eamon Melaugh, another radical, hoped that a provocation would ensue and boasted signs that read "Class War, not Creed War," "Orange and Green Tories Out," and "Police State Here."[4]

Seemingly determined to accommodate them, Northern Ireland's Minister for Home Affairs, William Craig, refused to authorize a permit for the rally, but approximately 400 individuals, including four Labour Party members of Parliament (MPs), appeared on a dreary afternoon that soon proved memorable. As a television camera recorded events, members of the Royal Ulster Constabulary (RUC) waded into the crowd, beating marchers, including MPs Gerry Fitt, Austin Currie, and Eddie McAteer, while directing a water cannon at others. Demonstrators, for their part, hurled rocks and gasoline bombs at the police. The scenes of police battering Catholic marchers resulted in a propaganda defeat for Craig and Northern Ireland's government, which was based in Stormont, a district outside of Belfast.

Prime Minister Terence O'Neill, who was contending with hard-line critics in his Unionist Party, soon acknowledged in a television address that "Ulster stands at the crossroads."[5] While blaming a small band of agitators for having created the atmosphere that led to the unhappy developments in Derry, he warned that "the tinder for that fire in the form of grievances, real or imaginary, had been building up for years."[6] O'Neill noted that since taking office five years earlier, he had attempted "to heal some of the deep divisions in our community. I did so because I could not see how an Ulster divided against itself could hope to stand." He then asked if all concerned parties desired a thriving province that remained within the United Kingdom or "a place continually torn apart by riots and demonstrations and regarded by the rest of Britain as a political outcast?"[7]

While the NICRA considered O'Neill sincere and agreed to suspend its demonstrations, the more militant People's Democracy called for a lengthy procession from Belfast to Derry, to be initiated on January 1, 1969. The march, a spokesman for the People's Democracy declared, would seek to duplicate the one undertaken by American civil rights activists from Selma to Montgomery in 1965, prior to congressional passage of that year's epochal Voting Rights Act. As the Irish marchers approached Derry, they encountered hundreds of loyalists who greeted them with bricks and rocks. Activist Bernadette Devlin stated that "hordes of screaming people" attacked both male and female marchers with "planks of wood, bottles, laths, iron bars, crowbars, cudgels studded with nails, and ... waded into the march beating the hell out of everybody."[8] Television cameras again relayed images of the beatings, with the police appearing to stand aside as the demonstrators were pummeled. On hearing about the incident, Catholics in the Bogside rioted, fighting the RUC, with hundreds suffering injuries. O'Neill blamed the People's Democracy activists for "a foolhardy and irresponsible undertaking." The Northern Ireland leader dismissed some marchers and their supporters as "mere hooligans ready to attack the police and others."[9]

In August 1969, a parade by the loyalist Apprentice Boys of Derry resulted in three days of clashes in the Bogside, pitting Catholics against Protestants. Attempting to overcome barricades and encountering petrol bombs and bricks, the RUC employed CS gas (also known as tear gas) and tossed back stones but the rioting continued. When the police managed to push through certain barricades, mobs of Protestants attacked the homes of Catholic residents. The all-but-universal anger within the Bogside led one priest to report, "I would only regard it as a community in revolt rather than just a street disturbance or a riot." In fact, conditions threatened to spiral out of control, with Belfast also soon erupting in violence when efforts were undertaken "to take the heat off the Bogside."[10]

On August 14, Inspector General Joseph Anthony Peacock of the RUC, fearing that war could break out, urged the deployment of British soldiers in Northern Ireland. Although British Prime Minister Harold Wilson and Home Secretary James Callahan were reluctant to issue such an order, envisioning a quagmire, they finally committed the troops. Initially, Catholic nationalists welcomed the soldiers, and tensions abated. Eight people had perished, with over 700 suffering injuries and nearly 200 houses and other buildings destroyed. Increasingly, Catholics anticipated support from the IRA but it generally was not forthcoming. Nevertheless, Citizens' Defence committees, supported by the IRA, appeared, seeking to safeguard Catholic districts against police or army assaults. However, at this stage few individuals in Catholic residential areas possessed weapons, which supporters in the Republic proved unable or unwilling to provide. Consequently, the IRA soon splintered, with the more militant Provisionals, in contrast to the Official IRA, demanding more concerted action; they soon acquired arms, thanks in part to American benefactors. Declaring that the Belfast government was "no longer in control of the situation," Jack Lynch, prime minister of the 26 Southern Counties, warned, "It is clear ... that the Irish Government can no longer stand by and see innocent people injured, and perhaps worse."[11] Lynch also indicated that he was stationing soldiers near the border with Northern Ireland, where they would set up field hospitals.

Within a short while, the British army, proving ill-equipped to police the Bogside, alienated the local population, whose residents, like those in the Creggan, sought to barricade themselves physically from the outside. As Pringle and Jacobson note, Irish Catholics set up fortifications, made "of rubble, slabs of concrete, old bedsteads, iron girders, planks of wood with rusty nails, burnt-out trucks and cars."[12] Republican-spearheaded street organizations, such as the Derry Citizens' Defence Committee, established greater control over the Bogside and other nationalist communities. In fact, those heavily barricaded and patrolled districts were said to be part of "Free Derry" and were referred to as "No-Go areas" by British forces, to the chagrin of unionists.[13] "Radio Free Derry," known as the "Voice of Liberation," urged residents to "join your vigilante patrols."[14] A large-scale riot erupted following a republican parade on Easter day 1970, leading to clashes with British soldiers. That incident resulted in the IRA's decision to threaten those forces, while the British army reasoned that the Catholic population of Derry had to be contained within the Bogside. During the summer of 1970, Provisionals in Derry, while seeking to construct a bomb in the Creegan, blew themselves up, along with two young girls. That August, following riots, the IRA shot at British soldiers for the first time in Derry, but weapons remained hard to come by. Bombings by the IRA began in September, with an electrical substation in Derry targeted.

Confrontations continued over the course of the next several months, which resulted in the fatal shootings of several young Irish Catholics, which inflamed the Bogside and the Creggan. John Taylor, Minister of State for Home Affairs, warned, "I would defend without hesitation the action taken by the Army authorities in Derry against subversives during the past week or so when it was necessary in the end to actually shoot to kill. I feel that it may be necessary to shoot even more in the forthcoming months in Northern Ireland."[15] During the early morning hours of August 9, 1971, Operation Demetrius began, as thousands of troops and police poured into Catholic ghettoes in Derry and Belfast, searching for nearly 500 suspects. Over

340 arrests followed, with the IRA's Gerry Adams, then a young militant, among those caught up in the dragnet, which initiated the practice of *internment*, allowing for suspects to be imprisoned without trial. The destruction of several homes followed, suspects endured prolonged interrogations featuring sensory deprivation, and gunfire filled the air, leading to 15 deaths, including that of Hugh Mullan, a Catholic priest. At this stage, only Catholics experienced the internment that British officials increasingly relied on. Tensions heightened in both Derry and Belfast, with IRA volunteers patrolling the barricades that ringed Catholic districts.

Following the events of early August 1971, the government refused to authorize any marches in Northern Ireland, but the NICRA indicated that it would conduct one in Derry on January 31, 1972. Although advised by the RUC to allow the march to proceed and then prosecute its leaders, Major General Robert Ford, who headed British forces in Northern Ireland, was determined to keep the march within the barricades or arbitrary border that cut off the Bogside from the rest of Derry. Boasting a population of approximately 55,000, Derry stood as Northern Ireland's second largest city, with two-thirds of its inhabitants residing in either the Bogside or the Creggan. For the previous two years, the IRA had effectively policed the Bogside, which infuriated British security forces and Unionists. In late October, General Ford had ordered Brigadier Andrew MacLellan to reestablish law and order in the Creggan and the Bogside. Instead, Catholics devised still more barricades. To Ford's dismay, the expanse of the No-Go areas increased, which led to the closing of serveral commercial enterprises.

By early January, Ford determined that "the minimum force necessary to achieve a restoration of law and order is to shoot ringleaders among the Derry Young Hooligans." Ford also worried that the IRA was increasingly making its presence felt in Derry. Already pressured by business operators, the government in Stormont, and British officials, Ford was distressed to hear from Brigadier MacLellan that the "The Front," which marked the No-Go area's northern boundary, would soon be encroaching on residential districts and would endanger Derry's major shopping area. In addition, Ford believed that batons, rubber bullets, and CS gas no longer sufficed to control the young hooligans who continually wreaked havoc in commercial centers. Ford again reasoned that law and order could only be restored if his forces targeted "selected ringleaders among the DYH, after clear warnings have been issued."[16] A week before the scheduled march of January 31, hundreds of British troops roughed up demonstrators outside an internment camp located in Magilligan, close to Derry. Seeking to prevent a similar development in Derry, the NICRA highlighted the need for an uneventful day.

On January 25, General Ford directed Brigadier MacLellan to make sure that the march in Derry was controlled. An Operation Order called for the construction of 26 barriers to divide the Bogside and the Creggan from Derry as a whole. Ford also ordered Lieutenant Colonel Derek Wilford, who headed the 1st Battalion Parachute Regiment, to Derry, along with the elite Paras. All the while, NICRA organizers remained uncertain about how to respond to the moves by British security forces. Additionally, both wings of the IRA, although worried that the march might result in British troops storming into the Bogside and the Creggan, refused to commit their own troops; the Provisionals and the Officials feared that a firefight could lead to civilian casualties. Meanwhile, Brigadier MacLellan, in directives delivered on January 27, stated that "the Containment Line and the area within it are to be dominated by physical military presence."[17]

Although John Hume feared violence would erupt and consequently refused to participate, the actual march began uneventfully on the early afternoon of Sunday, January 31. The crowd appeared festive, sporting a civil rights banner with its blue and white colors. Workers and professionals, men and women, teenagers and young children were in attendance. So too were both Eamonn McCann and Bernadette Devlin, the People's

Democracy leader who had been elected to Parliament in 1969. Shortly before 3:00 P.M., marshals argued with youngsters, the so-called hooligans who were determined to fight British soldiers. Soon, the troops employed rubber bullets and water cannon, enabling the Paras to conduct its clean-up operation.

Around 4:10, the Paras began firing on demonstrators. The shooting continued for 20 minutes, resulting in the greatest number of civilian casualties on Irish soil caused by British troops in the twentieth century. The coroner of Derry reported, "I say it without reservation—it was sheer, unadulterated murder."[18] However, the Widgery Tribunal report examining the causes of Bloody Sunday, released in April, largely absolved British troops of blame, to the indignation of Catholic nationalists. Over three decades later, repeated efforts were undertaken to determine precisely how events had unfolded on January 31, 1972. The immediate aftermath of Bloody Sunday was explosive, with more Catholics and Protestants joining paramilitary organizations and violence in Northern Ireland surging to its highest level during the period of the Troubles. On the floor of the House of Commons, MP Devlin, crying out that Home Secretary Reginald Maulding was a murderer, raced over to physically attack him, while in Dublin, the British embassy went up in smoke after an incendiary attack.

The poet Thomas Kinsella produced "Butcher's Dozen," his ode to those who had fallen on Bloody Sunday.

> Here lies one in blood and bones,
> Who lost his life for throwing stones....
> This lesson in our hearts we keep:
> Persuasion, protest, arguments,
> The milder forms of violence,
> Earn nothing but polite neglect.
> England, the way to your respect
> Is via murderous force, it seems;
> You push us to your own extremes.[19]

Bloody Sunday demonstrated the continued difficulty of

trying to carve out arbitrary borders in Northern Ireland. Those efforts, which including establishing political, cultural, and religious barriers, had proven futile. Physical structures, including actual barricades, were no more successful, as the sectarian divisions separating Irish Catholics and Protestants refused to abate. Those same structures, intended to secure such divisions, also demonstrated the failure of British policy, which seemingly sought to maintain colonial control in the midst of ever-increasing demands by Irish Catholics for political, cultural, and religious autonomy.

2

The English
Takeover

Blessed with a rich green countryside and a moderate, moist climate, Ireland boasts lowland wooded areas, rolling agrarian land, and peat bogs; mountains soaring as high as 3,400 feet; lakes; and exquisite coastal regions. The 26 Counties that make up the Republic of Ireland span 27,000 square miles; the 6 Counties of Northern Ireland sweep across a landscape about one-fifth that size. Bordered by the Atlantic Ocean on the south, west, and north, Ireland is separated from Wales and England by St. George's Channel and the Irish Sea, and from Scotland and northern England by the North Channel. Much of Northern Ireland was separated from the South by geographically defined borders, including "mountains, drumlins, forests and water," along with "the prehistoric earthworks known as the Black Pig's Dyke" that served as "the nearest Irish equivalent of Hadrian's Wall."[20]

Chroniclers contend that the initial inhabitants of Ireland probably arrived from Scotland around 7500 B.C.E. (before the Common Era). These Mesolithic people survived by hunting and fishing along Ireland's northeastern sector, with ancient settlements reaching down to County Cork. By 3500 B.C.E., Neolithic settlers, again probably of Scottish origin, established agriculturally based communities, while also constructing elaborate burial sites. Both the Bronze Age and the Iron Age subsequently came to Ireland, along with *Celtic* tribes that occupied parts of Spain, France, and Great Britain between the sixth and the fourth centuries B.C.E. A Gaelic civilization resulted, with southern and northern tribes controlling different sectors of Ireland. (The word *Gaelic* refers to the language and customs of the Celtic people.) The Gaelic influence remained strong, linguistically, legally, and economically, in the midst of seemingly constant battles waged by some 150 kingdoms. While priests administered religious practices, lawyers called brehons devised an intricate legislative code rooted in local communities and extended families. Rurally based Ireland exhibited a stratified social order that established cultural borders, with more than 20 classes of freemen and with women possessing considerable status.

Learning was greatly respected, as poets were both admired and feared for their satirical attacks. Considered warlike, the Irish conducted assaults at various times against England and Wales.

In the fifth century C.E. (Common Era), a former slave, Saint Patrick, helped to convert the Irish to Christianity and to introduce the Roman alphabet and Latin scholarship. As Irish monasteries flourished, missionaries sought to preach the gospel throughout much of Europe. Then in 795, Vikings conducted raids along Irish coastal areas, eventually establishing fortified settlements and the country's initial towns, including Cork, Dublin, and Waterford. Finally, in 1014, the Irish high king Brian Boru, after being named "emperor ... of the Irish," defeated the Vikings at the battle of Clontarf, close to Dublin.[21] Boru's death, however, prevented a unified kingdom from remaining in place. Clashes continued between the Irish and the Vikings, who increasingly were incorporated into Ireland's general population.

After the high king Turlough O'Connor defeated Diarmuid MacMurrough, king of Leinster, the ousted noble sought assistance from the *Normans* (who began the conquest of England in 1066) to regain his throne in the southeast. Thanks to their help, MacMurrough reacquired his kingdom in 1170 but died the following year, when he was replaced by a Norman baron, Richard FitzGerald de Clare, also known as Strongbow. As other Norman lords, boasting armor, horses, and fortified castles, took control of Irish land, English King Henry II (reign 1154–1189) went to Ireland in 1171 to ensure that those nobles and many Irish lords paid homage to him; Henry believed he was so entitled because of a papal bull by Adrian IV that seemingly awarded Ireland to the English monarch. In Ireland, the Normans planted *feudalism*, a European legal and administrative system founded on the exchange of reciprocal undertakings of protection and loyalty that highlighted *primogeniture*, which enabled first-born children (usually sons) to inherit all property rights and titles. Taking over great expanses of territory, the Normans, by the middle of the thriteenth century, controlled the vast majority of the Irish landscape. Western Ulster remained an exception to this phenomenon, which saw Norman lords fiercely seek to prevent royal interference with the operation of their estates. To the delight of most Irish clergy and the dismay of Edward II (reign 1307–1327), soldiers, led by Edward, brother of the Scottish king Robert the Bruce, invaded Ireland.

The willingness of Normans to adapt to Irish ways eventually troubled the English crown, which also worried about the reduced size of the *Pale*, the fortified arbitrary border around Dublin that was controlled by English officials. Steadily, the Normans became culturally assimilated, learning the Irish language, intermarrying with the Irish, and acquiring Gaelicized names. Consequently, in 1366, English officials, led by the Duke of Clarence, the son of Edward II, devised the Statutes of Kilkenny, which sought to prevent Anglo-Normans from speaking Irish, engaging in intermarriage with the Irish, employing their dress, accepting their laws, or even participating in the Irish sport of hurling (which involved throwing or carrying a ball to a goal some distance away). This set of artificially drawn cultural and religious shackles also mandated that "no Irish ... be admitted ... to any benefice of Holy Church among the English of the land ... and that no house of religion which is situated among the English ... receive any Irishmen." Few adhered to the Statutes, which attempted to devise "racial barriers," while Richard II (reign 1377–1399), during the last part of the fourteenth century, made two attempts, both unsuccessful, to solidify English rule in Ireland.[22] That rule became more lax still when Anglo-Norman knights departed from Ireland to join in battles in England during the Hundred Years War (1338–1453).

At various stages, English officials attempted to tighten their control over Ireland and the Irish population. In 1454, the Council in Dublin demanded the ouster of "al maner of men of Iryshe blode and women," who had resided within the city for fewer than a dozen years.[23] Violators of the edict were to be imprisoned. The following year, the Council affirmed that not only lay persons, but also Irish clergy and nuns were similarly proscribed from residing inside Dublin's walls. Outside the

Pale, however, the Irish resurgence continued, particularly in northern and western sectors. In 1494, Poynings' Law was proclaimed, requiring England to approve of acts passed by the Irish Parliament. Then, during the monarchy of Henry VIII (reign 1509–1547), the English quashed a rebellion led by the powerful Fitzgerald clan from Kildare. That enabled Henry VIII, who broke away from the Roman Catholic Church, to take control of the Irish Church and to proclaim himself King of Ireland. Mary I (reign 1553–1558) favored the setting up of English-run plantations in the Irish midlands, confiscating land in both Leix and Offaly counties.

Elizabeth I (reign 1558–1603) presided over the solidifying of English dominance of Ireland. Following the lead of her father, Henry VIII, Elizabeth tried to transplant Protestantism to Ireland, banning the holding of religious services by Roman Catholics and calling for the execution of several bishops and priests. Embittered resistance produced drawn-out wars in various instances, leading to "scorched earth policies" in Munster that resulted in mass bloodletting and famine. Eventually, anger over English practices under Elizabeth helped to produce, as Marcus Tanner indicates, "a common hatred of Protestantism." That in turn brought about "a new nationalism."[24] The final uprising during Elizabeth's reign occurred in Ulster in 1595, led by Hugh O'Neill of Tyrone, who in turn was backed by Catholic clergy. O'Neill reached out to Catholic Spain, which had recently suffered a terrible blow when many of the ships in its famed Armada were bested by inclement weather and English crewmen. After winning a pair of major battles, O'Neill suffered defeat at Kinsale in 1603, resulting in the quashing of Gaelic Ireland. Like Rory O'Donnell of Tyrconnel, O'Neill subsequently departed for the continent in the Flight of the Earls.

England now held sway over the whole of Ireland, with English law even supplanting Gaelic traditions in Ulster. In a concerted effort to strengthen that control by producing religiously rooted ethnic boundaries, James I (reign in Scotland 1567–1625; reign in England 1603–1625) supported the settlement of

English and Scottish Protestants in northern Ireland and other pockets around the country. The new settlers, designed "to serve as permanent watchmen," received some two million acres of rich land in west Ulster alone, leaving the native Irish with about a million acres of lesser quality upland territory.[25] Plantations also appeared in east Ulster, as did a haughty sense

THE FLIGHT OF THE EARLS

Beginning in the early sixteenth century, the English crown attempted to ensure that artificial boundaries would result in the subjugation of Ireland, acting to curb the reign of Gaelic lords and powerful figures descended from Anglo-Norman conquerors. Near the close of the century, only Ulster remained outside the English fold. There, Hugh O'Neill, the second Earl of Tyrone, along with Hugh O'Donnell, Lord of Tyrconnel, and Hugh Maguire of Fermanagh, battled against English forces. Brought up by an English nobleman and named Earl of Tyrone in 1587, O'Neill nevertheless refused to execute Spanish sailors following the defeat of the Spanish Armada and he soon began contesting English rule. O'Neill found safe haven in lush, western Ulster, with its natural barriers and lack of English colonialists and forts. In 1593, O'Neill took on the title of "The O'Neill," a prohibited Gaelic title, and acquired the backing of other Ulster chieftains.

Armed resistance started in 1595, with O'Neill triumphing in a number of early battles, including at Yellow Ford, close to Monaghan. With Spanish support, O'Neill undertook a 300-mile march to Kinslae in Cork, where his men were roundly defeated by a 12,000-man English contingent. O'Connell fled to Spain, where he subsequently died, and was succeeded as Lord of Tyrconnel by his brother Rory. O'Neill fought gamely for two additional years but agreed to sign a treaty at Mellifont in 1603, officially ending the Nine Years War. Oppressed by English authorities and their spies, O'Neill and Rory O'Donnell, along with their families and allies, left Ireland in 1607. After rough seas compelled them to land in France, they made their way to Rome, arriving in 1608. O'Neill died there in 1616. Back in Ireland, the Flight of the Earls, as the departure of O'Neill and O'Donnell came to be known, had enabled the English government to take control of six of Ulster's Nine Counties, thus resulting in new artificial barriers of a political nature.

of superiority that the settlers brought with them. While James I and Charles I (reign 1625–1649) initially allowed other Catholic landowners to retain their properties, provided tax revenues were collected, Charles eventually violated his promises after concerns about possible Spanish incursions lessened.

Charles ultimately confronted challenges to his autocratic rule in Scotland, England, and Ireland. The Gaelic Irish initially rebelled against Charles in 1641, worrying that imperial policies imperiled Catholicism's existence in Ireland. The religious divide heightened in Ireland, with Catholic perceptions providing the seeds for "a new Irish nationalism" based on "common allegiance to Catholicism."[26] Along the way, church desecrations and sectarian killings occurred, with many Protestants suffering at the hands of vengeful Catholics. Then in 1649, Oliver Cromwell (reign 1653–1658), who orchestrated a revolt that led to Charles's execution, determined to tackle the Irish dilemma in a manner no English ruler previously had, calling for the relocation of property-owning Catholics to barren Connacht. In the process, thousands of Irish starved daily, as almost 70 percent of Ireland's best land was turned over to Protestants, where it largely remained for 300 years. Following the death of Cromwell in 1658 and the ouster of his son and successor Richard (reign 1658–1659) the next year, some privileged Catholic families reacquired their estates. Throughout this period, famine, plague, and butchery beset the population of Ireland.

In 1685, the Catholic James II became king of England but was ousted three years later by William of Orange. James fled to Ireland, where he was warmly received by his fellow Catholics who joined his army, which was futilely striving to reestablish his throne. William defeated James in mid-1690 at the Battle of the Boyne, outside Drogheda, and the last of the deposed king's forces were bested a year later at the Battle of Aughrim, close to Galway. The Treaty of Limerick concluded the war, promising equitable treatment for Catholic soldiers and civilians. While the Catholic army was allowed to depart for France, in the so-called Flight of the Wild Geese, William's supporters in Ireland soon codified into law—through the devising of statutory barriers or borders—the so-called Protestant Ascendancy. The Penal Laws required members of Parliament to take an oath that condemned Catholic religious beliefs, insisted that Catholics not bear arms or possess horses valued at greater than five pounds, precluded parents from sending children to the continent to acquire a Catholic education, and demanded that all Catholic clergy depart from Ireland. The right of Catholics to practice law was restricted, along with their ability to purchase, inherit, or rent land. By the first decade of the eighteenth century, Catholics retained control of a mere 14 percent of the land in Ireland, while in Ulster, that amount was only 5 percent. The satirist and Protestant cleric, Jonathan Swift, Dean of Dublin's St. Patrick's Cathedral, produced Irish Tracts that urged the Irish to "Burn everything from England except her coal." He drafted a letter "to the 'Whole People of Ireland,'" indicating he was their "countryman, fellow-subject and fellow-sufferer."[27] Charles Duff suggests that Swift helped to usher in Protestant nationalism in Ireland.

During the last stages of the eighteenth century, sectarianism continued to afflict Ireland, along with seemingly perennial gang warfare. Following clashes in County Armagh in the mid-1780s, the Peep o'Day Boys, (so called from visits to the houses of loyalists at daybreak in search of arms), a Protestant group, and the Defenders, a Catholic organization, were organized. The Peep o'Day Boys set afire a Catholic church in Portadown, while the Defenders retaliated by torturing the family of a Protestant schoolteacher in Forkhill. Finally, on June 12, 1795, the Battle of the Diamond began, involving shootings between the two gangs. The battle continued intermittently for several months, eventually culminating in an ambush on September 21 when the Peep o'Day men murdered at least 30 Defenders. A militant, anti-Catholic front, the Orange Order, emerged out of this confrontation, determined to root out so-called disloyalists, whether they were Catholics or Protestants. In the fall of 1795, Orangemen forced thousands of Catholic families out of north

County Armagh, leading many to link up with the staunchly republican and revolutionary Society of United Irishmen.

Influenced by the American Revolution, Irish Protestants expressed increasing discontent with British control during the last decades of the eighteenth century. In 1782, the all-Protestant Irish Volunteers appeared, declaring "that as men and as Irishmen, as Christians and as Protestants, we rejoice in the relaxation of the Penal laws against our Roman Catholic fellow-subjects."[28] That same year, the Irish parliament, based in Dublin, acquired virtual independence, with Ireland standing as a kingdom apart from England, with which it shared a monarch. Henry Grattan, praised by another MP as "the father of the independence of this Country," asserted that the Irish people were "free," and remained tied to England through both allegiance and "liberty."[29] Grattan led the fight for legislative autonomy and soon successfully urged repeal of the vast bulk of the Penal Laws that had restricted the rights of Catholics, but had also been directed against Presbyterians in northern counties.

The French Revolution also influenced events in Ireland, resulting in the formation in 1791 of the United Irishmen, which was headed by Theobald Wolfe Tone, an attorney from Dublin. The new organization particularly appealed to Scottish Presbyterians in Ulster. A Protestant, Tone produced a stirring pamphlet, *An Argument on behalf of the Catholics of Ireland,* which insisted that liberty would not be found on the island until "Irish of all denominations" joined together to oppose the "boobies and blockheads" who controlled imperial policy.[30] Tone urged separation from England and the unification of the "Protestant, Catholic and Dissenter"—the ending of divisive religious barriers—under the banner of "Irishman."[31] Thus, Tone was committed to eradicating the arbitrary colonial boundaries that England had crafted for his home country.

The war between Britain and revolutionary France that began in 1793 drove the United Irishmen underground, with British authorities conducting a particularly brutal search for the rebels in 1796, following the appearance of French ships off the coast of Ireland. Anticipating an insurrection, British officials again resorted to heavy-handed practices the following year, while seeking to disarm the United Irishmen. Backed by the Church of Ireland, Tone finally triggered an armed revolt in 1798 that was put down, notwithstanding aid the rebels received from France. Convicted of treason and sentenced to hang, the imprisoned Tone committed suicide instead, becoming a sainted figure in Irish republican circles. His rebellion was brutally suppressed in both east Ulster and Wexford, where it had temporarily thrived.

Responding to events in Ireland, British Prime Minister William Pitt helped bring about the passage in 1800 of the Act of Union, which established the United Kingdom of Great Britain and Ireland. Because of this arbitrary creation, which sought to terminate actual national borders, the Irish parliament dissolved, with Ireland now sending representatives to *Westminster*, site of the British parliament. Another rebellion soon broke out in Ireland, this one led by United Irishman Robert Emmet, another Protestant from Dublin, who desired to create an Irish republic. As he awaited his execution, Emmet defiantly declared, "Let no man write my epitaph.... When my country takes her place among the nations of the earth, then, and not til then, let my epitaph be written."[32] The British government also viewed the Orange Order as endangering public order, and banned the organization in 1825.

Determined to achieve political freedom for his fellow Catholics, the lawyer Daniel O'Connell established the Irish Catholic Association in 1823, which sought Irish emancipation. After O'Connell's election to Parliament in 1828, the British government abandoned the requirement that MPs adhere to the Oath of Supremacy, which proclaimed the monarch head of the established church. However, many of the supporters of the "Liberator," as O'Connell was called, were effectively disfranchised when property requirements for voters were sharply increased. O'Connell, who became lord mayor of Dublin in 1841, held a series of mass rallies urging repeal of the Act of Union, while always professing loyalty to Queen Victoria. The

British government, for its part, continued to view O'Connell as a threat, with Prime Minister Robert Peel indicting him, along with other top figures associated with the repeal movement, for conspiracy. Convicted, O'Connell was incarcerated in Richmond prison. Shortly thereafter, however, the House of Lords overturned the court decision, resulting in a great celebration in Dublin.

Partially to counter O'Connell's popularity, Prime Minister Peel decided to sponsor reform in Ireland, including the establishment of a series of non-denominational colleges, along with Trinity College in Dublin, across Ireland. O'Connell's opposition to the plan helped to further distance him from a number of young, militant nationalists, who supported cultural nationalism, established the *Nation* newspaper, and joined the Young Ireland movement. As Brian Feeney notes, the movement's founders were attracted "to the German concept of Volksgeist, the idea that every nationality has a spirit or a 'genius' peculiar to its people."[33] In the midst of a series of revolutions on the continent in 1848, the movement attempted an aborted uprising of its own but that proved to be a futile undertaking.

Ireland, by that point, had suffered the death of one million people, owing to disease and famine, caused by a potato blight that the British government refused to attempt to alleviate. A similar number of Irish citizens left for the United States, while others emigrated to Britain, Canada, and Australia. Beginning in 1845, a fungus ravaged the potato crop, which the vast majority of desperately poor Irish inhabitants relied on as a staple of their diet. Notwithstanding the outbreak of the potato famine, the English government, with its free market approach, refused to provide economic assistance, even as foodstuffs were exported out of Ireland. The failure of Queen Victoria to respond to the tragedy that unfolded in Ireland helped to dampen Catholic royalism (proponents of which remained loyal to the British crown). In the United States, embittered Irish immigrants remained hostile to the British government.

The staunchly pro-Unionist Orange Order, with lodges found

in Scotland, England, and Canada, resurfaced as a political force by the middle of the nineteenth century. During that same period, two members of the Young Ireland movement, James Stephens and Thomas Clark Luby, established the Irish Republican Brotherhood (IRB), a secret group that had support both in Ireland and the United States and condemned the artificially created Act of Union. IRB members were known as Fenians, hearkening back to old Celtic fighters, the *Fianna*. The Catholic Church condemned the Fenians, but many younger clergy furtively backed them. The membership oath of the Fenians contained a salute to "the Irish Republic, now virtually established" and their proclamation of 1867 affirmed, "We therefore declare that, unable longer to endure the curse of Monarchical government, we aim at founding a Republic based on universal suffrage, which shall secure to all the intrinsic value of their labour."[34] The Fenians conducted an aborted uprising in 1867 and became the first Irish republicans to plant bombs in England. Soon, the Fenians were forced underground, but they continued to attempt to influence other organizations, including the Land League and the Gaelic Athletic Association (GAA), which had strong backing from the Fenians.

Michael Davitt, a former Fenian who favored the nationalization of land, and Charles Stewart Parnell, a Protestant landlord, founded the Irish National Land League in 1879. Relying on boycotts, the Land League sought to empower poorer tenants. Eventually, Parnell dominated the organization, pushing for the passage of Land Acts that deeded property to tenants. Considered Ireland's uncrowned monarch, Parnell favored *Home Rule*, which would have established a dual house legislative body in Dublin while keeping Ireland within the United Kingdom. By the mid-1880s, Parnell received almost unanimous support from the Irish Catholic Church. In 1886, Prime Minister William Gladstone offered a Home Rule bill, which produced virtually unanimous opposition among Ulster's Protestants and revitalized the Orange Order. Speaking on behalf of the proposed legislation and seeking to end all artificial borders afflicting Ireland, Parnell informed the House of Commons, "We want the energy, the patriotism, the talent, and works of every Irishman to make this great experiment ... successful.... We want ... all creeds and all classes in Ireland. We cannot look upon a single Irishman as not belonging to us."[35]

However, as the bill failed, sectarian battles rifled through Belfast and other northern communities, with riots resulting in scores of deaths. The violence reinforced the determination of Ulster's Protestants to oppose Home Rule. A sexual scandal destroyed Parnell's reputation, as the Catholic Church turned against him, and John Redmond replaced him as the leading Irish nationalist. Now heading the Irish Parliamentary Party (IPP) that Parnell had founded, Redmond also favored Home Rule, as did his supporters, the National Volunteers. In 1893, Gladstone again futilely proposed passage of a Home Rule Bill.

Meanwhile, a Gaelic revival took hold, spearheaded initially by the GAA, which sought to highlight the ancient sport of hurling, along with European-style football. In 1893, the Protestant writer Douglas Hyde established the Gaelic League, which strove to reestablish interest in the Irish language. Indeed, Irish initially was not taught in public schools in Ireland. Hyde fought to have Irish become a required subject for those seeking entrance to the National University in Dublin. An Englishwoman, Annie Horniman, helped to establish the Irish National Theatre, also in Ireland's major city. Among those soon associated with the National Theatre were the poet-playwright W.B. Yeats and the playwright J.M. Synge, author of *The Playboy of the Western World*.

From the first incursions ordered by the English crown in the twelfth century, efforts to subjugate the Irish had been employed. These at first involved military, political, and economic controls, but eventually included cultural ones. However, restrictive legislation and oppressive policies failed to prevent Gaelic cultural influences from resurfacing. Eventually, following the advent of the Protestant Reformation, England attempted to subjugate

Irish Catholics militarily, while resorting to heavy-handed immigration policies, in which entire groups of Scottish and English colonists were transplanted to Ireland. Property, franchise, and other legal restrictions afflicted the native Catholic population, which fought back at various intervals. Along with Protestant rebels and radicals influenced by eighteenth- and nineteenth-century revolutions, Catholics battled for a Irish republic in different guises, sometimes of an absolute sort and, at other points, but a pale imitation of a genuine nation. Nevertheless, as the twentieth century approached, both political and cultural nationalism associated with the breaking down of artificial boundaries appeared to be flourishing in Ireland, to the dismay of many British officials and Irish Protestants, particularly in Ulster.

3

The Battle
for Home Rule

As the struggle to achieve Home Rule foundered, Arthur Griffith, in the opening stages of the twentieth century, strove to foster greater political unity and organization for disparate nationalist strains first appearing over half-a-century earlier; he was determined to contest the arbitrary colonial barriers afflicting Ireland. In the pages of his newspaper, *United Irishman,* and in other publications, Griffith suggested that the culturally rooted Irish Ireland movement offered too little, an assessment with which writers on the order of James Joyce and W.B. Yeats agreed. In 1900, Griffith founded Cumann na nGaedheal, which sought to further national independence for Ireland, while three years later, he set up a National Council to protest a visit by Edward VII to Dublin. Soon, he helped to establish Sinn Féin, which ultimately became, as Brian Feeney notes, "the political wing of the country's repblican movement."

Griffith favored the establishment of an independent Irish parliament and of continued allegiance, by both Britain and Ireland, to the same monarch. He urged such an approach, believing that most inhabitants of Ireland did not support the creation of a republic, which would end the now century-old artificial British Union. In July 1904, Griffith argued that Irish MPs—over 80 altogether—should abstain from sitting in Westminster; instead, they should convene in Dublin, boycott British administration, establish their own courts, and collect taxes. This idea is known as *absention.* He also called for a protectionist economic policy to safeguard Irish industry and manufacturing. Many of Griffith's ideas, including that of absention, appeared in his book, *The Sinn Féin Policy,* which came out in 1904, a time when nationalist movements were thriving in central and southern Europe.

The Irish Republican Brotherhood (IRB), which Griffith had joined, opposed his call for a dual monarchy, arguing that he failed to consider the inherently anti-Catholic bias of the British crown. Republicans, for their part, were no happier with Griffith's willingness to pay homage to the British monarchy, aspiring instead to Irish autonomy. Nevertheless, Griffith's ideas, Feeney suggests, resonated with many, as did the sensibility that *Sinn Féin* stood for various beliefs and behaviors associated with separatism or an Irish Ireland. Although lacking organizational structure, Sinn Féin represented a movement, as well as a political agenda.

Hoping to prevent Sinn Féin from becoming a fringe group, Griffith desired to welcome as many diverse viewpoints as possible, rather than only proposals for an Irish republic. As a result, however, many IRB members, both those seeking to use violence on the path to separatism and those desiring peaceful change through political processes, joined Sinn Féin. The IRB published *Irish Freedom,* which demanded a republican government for the entire island.

In 1910, a Liberal government headed by Prime Minister Herbert H. Asquith came to power in Britain, thanks to the backing of MPs from the Irish Parliamentary Party, including John Redmond. The British administration agreed to consider another Home Rule bill, which was bitterly opposed by Irish unionists, especially those in Ulster who were led by Sir Edward Carson, a Dublin-born attorney and member of the Church of Ireland, and his Irish Unionist Party. Carson also headed the Ulster Unionist Council (UUC), which condemned the idea of Home Rule. Another leader of the Unionist camp was the Presbyterian James Craig, an MP from East Down, who like Carson, belonged to the Orange Order. In early 1911, Craig declared that if necessary, northern Protestants would respond in the manner Lord Randolph Churchill predicted: "Ulster will fight, and Ulster will be right."[36] Before a massive rally outside Belfast in September 1911, Carson warned that if a Home Rule bill passed, "We must be prepared ... to take such measures as will enable us to carry on the government of those districts of which we have control. We must be prepared ... ourselves to become responsible for the government of the Protestant province of Ulster."[37]

In August 1911, in the midst of Parliamentary deliberations regarding Home Rule for Ireland, the possibility of partition was discussed; Parliament was turning to an arbitrary border as a solution to resolve the longstanding Irish dilemma. Clearly recognizing that it would prove unacceptable, Carson offered his own solution, which called for the separation of Ulster's Nine Counties from the rest of Ireland; Prime Minister Asquith rejected Carson's proposal, which itself demanded new arbitrary borders. During a cabinet meeting in February 1912, David Lloyd George, assisted by Winston Churchill, broached the idea of removing the Ulster counties from the Home Rule bill. Subsequently, Redmond agreed that the Nine Northern Counties should be allowed to avoid Home Rule for a brief period, but Unionists condemned this suggestion.

Following in dismay Parliament's deliberations on the Home Rule bill, Carson and Craig initiated a campaign by Ulster Protestants to support a petition opposing Home Rule. Their petition, the Solemn League and Covenant, which 200,000 to 500,000 Unionists signed, insisted "that home rule would be disastrous to the material well-being of Ulster as well as the whole of Ireland, subversive of our civil and religious freedom, destructive of our citizenship, and perilous to the unity of the Empire."[38] Carson affirmed that "if it be treason to love your King, to try to save your Constitution, to preserve your birthright, and your civil and religious liberty, then I glory in being a traitor."[39]

Unionists mobilized in other ways, too, forming the Ulster Volunteer Force (UVF), an armed militia with a membership of 100,000 by 1912; within two years, the UVF received 25,000 weapons, along with 3 million rounds of ammunition, from outside Ireland. Proponents of gradual independence responded by establishing the Irish Volunteer Force, which, like the UVF, illegally imported weapons—though not nearly as successfully as the Unionist organization—and conducted drills. The Irish Volunteers, headed by Eoin MacNeill, sought to ensure that the rights of all citizens of Ireland were safeguarded, regardless of religious belief, class standing, or political perspective. Nevertheless, the apparent strength of the UVF led Prime

Minister Asquith to acknowledge that "the instrument would break," if he tried to suppress the UVF militarily.[40] The British government undertook few efforts to halt the UVF's gunrunning escapades, but it sought to grab weapons headed for the Irish Volunteers outside Dublin in 1914. Frustrated British soldiers fired on an angry crowd, killing three civilians.

The Home Rule bill, which failed to offer dominion status to Ireland or autonomy regarding financial affairs, was to become effective in 1914, but its implementation was postponed, due to the outbreak of World War I. Most Irish citizens rallied to back Great Britain, with 35,000 Irish soldiers, both Catholics and Protestants, perishing in the conflict. Following Redmond's lead, most of the Irish Volunteers supported the war effort, but a contingent of 10,000 refused to do so. This group, the National Volunteers (henceforth referred to as the Volunteers), included IRB members and linked up with the newly created Citizen Army, a socialist group that championed separatism. The Citizen Army was headed by James Connolly, a former soldier and the founder of the Socialist Republican Party, and Jack White, an ex-British Army officer. Connolly reasoned that such a military force was necessary, following the brutal suppression of James Larkins's Irish Transport and General Workers' Union. Shortly after the war began, the IRB's supreme council determined that an insurrection must take place in Ireland before the conflict ended. The death in 1915 of Jeremiah O'Donovan Rosa, a staunch Fenian long incarcerated in British prisons, helped to trigger opposition to British actions. The poet and schoolteacher Padraig Pearse, who was a leader of both the Volunteers and the IRB, delivered a stirring eulogy. "Life springs from death; and from the graves of patriot men and women spring living nations," Pearse stated. He continued,

> The Defenders of this Realm have worked well in secret and in the open. They think they have pacified Ireland... They think that they have foreseen everything, think that they have provided against everything; but the fools, the fools, the fools!

They have left us our Fenian dead, and while Ireland holds these graves, Ireland unfree shall never be at peace.[41]

Over the span of several months, members of the IRB, operating through the Volunteers and the Citizen Army, readied for the insurrectionary action they had long envisioned. They were supported by women's auxiliary groups, headed by the likes of Countess Constance Markiewicz, an Irishwoman who was an officer of the Citizen Army. These would-be revolutionaries confronted formidable foes, including the highly trained, 10,000 man-strong Royal Irish Constabulary (RIC), which served as an armed police force and, almost without exception, fully supported British rule. The well-armed British Army remained as an occupying force in Ireland. On April 21, 1916, off the coast of Kerry, the British navy intercepted a shipment of 20,000 old Russian arms and a number of machine guns from Germany, an

HOME RULE

Following his initial appointment as prime minister of Great Britain in 1868, William Gladstone of the Liberal Party declared, "My mission is to pacify Ireland." After proceeding to deprive the Church of Ireland of its status and privileges, in a gesture of goodwill to the vast majority of the Irish people who were Catholics, Gladstone attempted land reform, to improve the condition of destitute tenants. In subsequent terms as prime minister, Gladstone struggled to contend with the demand for Home Rule, the movement demanding greater autonomy for Ireland within the British Commonwealth.

In 1870, Isaac Butt, a Protestant attorney, established the Home Government Association, which called for Irish MPs to retain their seats in Westminster but also urged the setting up of a parliament in Dublin that would be in charge of domestic affairs in Ireland. In 1873, the Home Rule League appeared, and within a year, 59 MPs supported Home Rule. By 1881, the Irish Parliamentary Party, favoring Home Rule, named Charles Stewart Parnell to head it. Fenian leaders, including Michael Davitt of the Land League illegal operation set up by Sir Roger Casement, previously a member of the British consular service. The interception resulted in a division within the ranks of the Volunteers, with some opposing a planned uprising scheduled for three days later and others, including Pearse, insisting that the action be carried out. The opposition, led by Eoin MacNeill, ultimately served as a fatal blow for both the Volunteers and the Nationalist Party, while strengthening the hand of the increasingly militant Sinn Féin.

On Easter Monday, April 24, 1916, 1,500 lightly armed members of the Volunteers and the Citizen Army, half possessing no weapons at all, gathered at Liberty Hall in normally tranquil Dublin. Reports later surfaced that Pearse and Connolly understood the suicidal nature of the Easter Rising, as the attempted revolt came to be known. No matter, they remained determined to provide a model for other patriots willing to sacrifice their

and John Devoy, who guided Clan na nGael, the Fenians' American branch, joined with Parnell to form an alliance called the "New Departure." The results of the 1885 General Elections, which demonstrated the political appeal of Home Rule, induced Gladstone, again serving as prime minister, to respond with his first, ultimately unsuccessful Home Rule bill.

A sexual scandal soon ended Parnell's political influence, but Gladstone remained committed to Home Rule, offering a second bill in 1893, which was also defeated, as its predecessor had been, by the House of Lords. Nevertheless, Gladstone's Liberal Party continued to support Home Rule and, joined by John Redmond's United Irish League, managed to curb the House of Lords' veto power. Thus, in 1911, another Home Rule bill was presented, which was slated to become effective in 1914. In Ireland, the new Unionist Party, a Protestant organization based in Ulster, remained bitterly opposed to Home Rule, fearing Protestants would be submerged in a Catholic Ireland. The outbreak of World War I caused Home Rule to be suspended, to the dismay of many Irish nationalists, many of whom now demanded full autonomy and an end to the artificial boundaries that the Act of Union had produced.

lives for independence. Pearse reasoned that "blood sacrifice" must redeem "the failure of the last generation."[42]

The rebels, isolated after Griffith and MacNeill canceled a series of campaigns scheduled to take place throughout Ireland, intended to grab hold of key sectors of Dublin, which they hoped the British would not dare to bomb. Pearse and Connelly set up their headquarters at the three-storied General Post Office, located on Sackville Street (later O'Connell Street). From there, a new flag, sporting green, white, and orange bars, now flew, while Pearse and Connolly produced a "Declaration of the Republic." Proclaiming the establishment of "the Provisional Government of the Irish Republic," Pearse and Connolly exclaimed,

> Irishmen and Irishwomen: In the name of God and of the dead generations from which she receives her old tradition of nationhood, Ireland, through us, summons her children to her flag and strikes for her freedom.... We declare the right of the people of Ireland to the ownership of Ireland and to the unfettered control of Irish destinies, to be sovereign and inde-feasible."[43]

Pearse took on the title of president of the Provisional Government.

Taken aback by the initial attacks, British officials soon responded by drawing on additional forces outside Dublin and demanding that reinforcements be sent from England. By Wednesday, April 26, the British forces outnumbered the insurgents 20 to 1, and called on artillery, which resulted in parts of Dublin becoming engulfed in flames. With a blockade in place, no food or water could be brought into the city. By Friday morning, Pearse reported, "The enemy has burnt down whole blocks of houses," but he asserted that the rebels had "redeemed Dublin from many shames" and "saved Ireland's honor."[44]

The fighting ended on Saturday, when Pearse and Connolly agreed to an unconditional surrender "to prevent the further slaughter of Dublin citizens."[45] The bitter, urban brawl left

The damage in Dublin was extensive during the Irish Republican Army's armed rebellion against British troops on Easter Day, 1916. This attempted revolt , known as the Easter Rising, was unsuccessful, but the execution of 16 leaders of the uprising produced support for Irish republicanism.

hundreds of British soldiers dead or wounded, along with some 1,000 Irish civilians and combatants. In an embittered letter to Sir Matthew Nathan, British Under-Secretary for Ireland, the great dramatist George Bernard Shaw asked,

> And why, oh why didn't the artillery knock down half Dublin whilst it had the chance. Think of the insanitary (sic) areas, the slums, the glorious chance of making a clean sweep of them! Only 179 houses and probably at least nine of them quite decent ones. I'd have laid at least 17,900 of them flat and made a decent town of it![46]

It was apparent that the uprising garnered sparse public

support, with many viewing it as a threat to the campaign for Home Rule or an affront to soldiers then serving on the continent. As they were taken away, prisoners heard crowds jeer and boo them. A harsher fate soon awaited many, particularly the ringleaders. In spite of Shaw's admonition against "canonizing their prisoners," British officials proceeded to do exactly that.[47] Determined to mete out severe punishment, the British government established martial law in Ireland and ordered the leaders of the rebellions to be tried by court martial and executed. During his court martial, Pearse warned, "We seem to have lost, we have not lost. To refuse to fight would have been to lose, to fight is to win, we have kept faith with the past and handed a tradition to the future."[48] Following the holding of secret trials, firings squads, operating over a 10-day span in early May, shot down 15 men, including Pearse and the severely wounded Connolly, who was suffering from gangrene and had to be placed on a chair so he could be executed. Others had death sentences commuted to prison terms. Constance Markievicz, Thomas Ashe, Eoin MacNeill, and Eamonn de Valera all received life sentences. The fact that de Valera had been born in the United States enabled him to avoid sharing the fate of Pearse, Connolly, Tom Clarke, Sean MacDiarmada, and other Easter Rising leaders.

On August 3, Roger Casement was hung. Before Casement was executed, Shaw warned, "You certainly did not find him a national hero. There is, however, one infallible way that can be done: and that way is to hang him."[49] On September 25, 1916, the poet William Butler Yeats completed *Easter 1916*, in which he sang out,

> We know their dream; enough
> To know they dreamed and are dead;
> And what if excess of love
> Bewildered them till they died?
> I write it out in a verse -
> MacDonagh and MacBride

And Connolly and Pearse
Now and in time to be,
Wherever green is worn,
Are changed, changed utterly:
A terrible beauty is born.[50]

The executions produced what the Easter Rising had failed to bring about: an outpouring of support for the republican cause and martyrdom for its ill-fated leaders. Anger mounted too, following reports that British soldiers had shot or bayoneted civilians during the Easter Rising. While declaring that civilians had been "killed by rebels and soldiers," Prime Minister Asquith insisted that it was "impossible" to ascertain the guilt of any specific individuals.[51] An inquiry, chaired by Baron Hardinge, commended most British officials involved with Ireland, and then applauded the British military, the Dublin police, and the RIC; the general Irish populace hardly received these findings happily.

Although British officials and soldiers crushed the Easter Rising, the memory of it and the treatment afforded some 2,000 prisoners, including the 16 men who were executed, lingered on, providing ammunition for the proponents of republicanism. While few Irish residents of Dublin or other parts of Ireland initially supported the rebels, their seemingly heroic acts, the apparent nobility they displayed in awaiting summary executions, and the insensitive response of the British government ultimately well served the cause the rebels espoused. While Pearse, Connolly, and other martyred figures received death sentences, the struggle for which they relinquished their lives continued, guided by many of the same individuals associated with the Easter Rising and its demand for an Irish republic. That battle and the memory of the Easter Rising leaders ensured that arbitrary borders of the mind existed, separating republicans from the British and Irish residents from one another.

4

The Irish
Revolution

The Easter Rising terminated the tenuous agreement by most Catholics and Protestants in Ireland to support the war effort. Fearing that the Easter Rising demonstrated what Home Rule could lead to, many Protestants fully backed the British troops who quashed the attempted revolt. By contrast, Catholics, including high church officials, refused to condemn the rebels. Following the execution of several of the Rising's leaders, Bishop Edward O'Dwyer from Limerick blasted the British government, charging, "Your regime has been one of the blackest chapters in the history of the misgovernment of" Ireland.[52] Then in July 1916, cabinet member David Lloyd George, acting at Prime Minister Asquith's behest, called for the immediate introduction of Home Rule with northeastern Ireland to remain under parliamentary control. Acceding to George's wishes, John Redmond of the Irish Parliamentary Party (IPP) convinced Joe Devlin, a leading IPP operative in the North, to support temporary partition. However, unionists demanded that Ulster avoid Home Rule, while southern Protestants and many Catholic nationalists attacked the proposal that would separate the Southern and Northern Counties or produce arbitrary borders of a seemingly permanent nature.

In a series of special elections, beginning in early 1917, candidates associated with a revitalized Sinn Féin, such as Eamon de Valera, won seats. Young clergy, who staunchly opposed partition, openly supported republican candidates, even those like de Valera, who had been imprisoned owing to his role as a military commander during the Easter Rising. During this same period, leaders from the IRB, such as Michael Collins and Thomas Ashe, helped to transform their organization, while garnering more support for a volunteer army dedicated to republican principles. In the midst of a hunger strike following his arrest, Ashe died when authorities attempted to forcibly feed him, thereby creating yet another martyr for Irish republicans.

Throughout 1917, the Irish Republican Brotherhood took control of Sinn Féin. On October 25, Sinn Féin held its annual convention, or *ard fheis*, in Dublin, with de Valera replacing

Arthur Griffith as president. Griffith, in fact, deferred to the younger man, declaring, "In Eamonn de Valera we have a soldier and a statesman."[53] Griffith and Father Michael O'Flanagan, a fiery priest who served on Sinn Féin's executive board, now served as the organization's vice-presidents, while Collins, another veteran of the Easter Rising, was Director of Organization. De Valera also became president of the Irish Volunteers. The new Sinn Féin was distinctly more radical than its predecessor, relying heavily on the Volunteers, who continued to champion the use of force to usher in a republic. A party manifesto called for Sinn Féin to employ any means to prevent England from subjugating Ireland. Thus, Sinn Féin abandoned support for a dual monarchy, which the IPP still backed, thereby ensuring a rift between the two groups.

As Sinn Féin's appeal seemed to spread like wildfire in the South, large portions of northern Ireland remained hostile to the organization's call for an Irish republic. The northeastern sector of Ireland continued to elect Unionist MPs, while the Catholic Church also opposed Sinn Féin's efforts in Ulster and the IPP remained a powerful competitor in that region. Sinn Féin's sustained backing of a policy of absention greatly disturbed many northern nationalists, who worried that it would only ensure that partition occurred. Those nationalists feared the establishment of arbitrary borders that would separate them from the rest of Ireland. Thus, hotly contested electoral contests took place in the Northern Counties, in which Sinn Féin and IPP candidates ran against one another, leading to a series of Sinn Féin defeats. Ulster unionists appeared unconcerned at this stage, believing that permanent partition was impending.

Now drawing on de Valera's leadership, Sinn Féin, by early 1918, grew more quickly than any other political movement in the history of Ireland, as Brian Feeney notes. By the spring, the number of Sinn Féin clubs in Ireland had mushroomed to 1,700, with an estimated membership of 120,000 to 130,000 in a country with fewer than 4.5 million people. However, Sinn Féin remained weak in many northeastern communities, even failing to dislodge the IPP in a number of Catholic districts. In many other sectors of Ireland, disaffected farmers and young laborers linked up with Sinn Féin, with a large number also joining the Volunteers. Women similarly flocked to Sinn Féin, as they did to Cumann na mBan, an auxiliary of the Volunteers. Recent electoral triumphs bolstered Sinn Féin's reputation, as did British actions. Sinn Féin necessarily benefited from the repressive actions of British authorities, which included the incarceration of thousands, and the poor treatment of those behind bars, culminating in the death of Ashe, head of the organization's Supreme Council. Ashe's martyrdom, Brian Feeney offers, proved catalytic, leading many to join Sinn Féin and the Volunteers and engage in revolutionary actions.

On April 16, 1918, the British passed a modification of the Conscription Act, extending its provisions to Ireland. Sinn Féin, the IPP, and the Labour Party all opposed the measure, as did Catholic clergy and trade unions in Ireland. Those groups spearheaded the opposition to the Conscription Act, with a general strike sweeping across Ireland, failing to take hold only in northeastern Ulster. Eventually, Prime Minister Lloyd George recognized that the Conscription Act could not be enforced, but the British government proved determined to go after those deemed most responsible for that setback. Beginning on May 17, British officials began responding to a supposed German conspiracy, which purportedly involved some 115 Sinn Féin leaders. These leaders were now rounded up along with over 1,300 other Irish men and women, including several individuals who had previously been indicted following the Easter Rising, such as de Valera, Griffith, and Countess Markievicz. Determined to make a political statement, the Sinn Féin hierarchy allowed itself to be arrested. Those taken into custody were soon shipped off to England, where they were interned. The British government insisted that the Sinn Féin detainees were not being held because of their opposition to the Conscription Act, but rather because they had been involved in a plot with Germany, Britain's leading wartime antagonist.

While the jailings seemingly weakened Sinn Féin, the Volunteers, despite de Valera's imprisonment, soon appeared more potent than ever. Moreover, the plight of their jailed comrades, viewed as political prisoners, only spurred compatriots in Ireland to maintain their struggle. Deemed "the most wanted in Ireland," Collins, who was devising an elaborate spy network, had a price on his head amounting to 10,000 pounds.[54] The arrest of Sinn Féin leaders further radicalized the republican movement, allowing figures like Collins to acquire greater standing still.

As the General Election of December 1918 approached, the imprisoned de Valera urged electoral support that would enable Irish representatives to attend the peace conference at Versailles and let Ireland take her proper place among the other nations of the world. Virtually sweeping the elections, Sinn Féin captured 73 seats to only 6 for the IPP and 26 for Unionists, all but 3 of those from Ulster. The election results only magnified the growing determination of Unionists to have much of Ulster partitioned from the rest of Ireland, which would solidify the presence of arbitrary borders. Sinn Féin leaders, on the other hand, continued to believe "that any division in the country was artificially created and partitionist feelings deliberatly fomented by the British."[55]

De Valera and 35 other successful candidates from Sinn Féin remained imprisoned, while all members of the organization refused to take their seats in Westminster. Instead, the available Sinn Féin representatives gathered in Dublin on January 21, 1919, where they held the first Dail Eireann, or Irish parliament, and issued a Declaration of Independence. The manifesto proclaiming the creation of an Irish Republic affirmed, "We solemnly declare foreign government in Ireland to be an invasion of our national right which we will never tolerate, and we demand the evacuation of our country by the English Garrison."[56] Following a dramatic escape from Lincoln prison in February, de Valera traveled to the United States, where he remained for the next year-and-a-half, soliciting funds for the Irish republicans. In the meantime, the Dail named de Valera

Eamon de Valera inspects members of the Western Division of the Irish Republican Army at Six Mile Bridge, Country Clare, during the Sinn Féin Rebellion.

president of the Irish Republic and selected a cabinet, which included Griffith, Markievicz, and MacNeill, as well as important military figures like Collins, Cathal Brugha, and Richard Mulcay. De Valera responded to his election by ensuring that Sinn Féin remained apart from the Dail.

On the same day as the convening of the Dail, January 21, 1919, Volunteers ambushed members of the Royal Irish Constabulary in County Tipperary, killing two. A brutal guerrilla campaign or the Irish War of Independence began, with the Volunteers serving as a national military force that later was renamed the *Irish Republican Army* (*IRA*). Headed by Collins, the IRA, which paid little heed to political leaders in Dublin, frequently lacked both arms and ammunition throughout the duration of the War of Independence. In mid-1919, shortly after the Versailles Peace Conference ended, the British government began to focus more fully on the situation in Ireland.

Over the next several months, British officials moved to ban both the Cumann na mBan and the Gaelic League. In late September, the British government announced that it viewed the Dail as illegal.

The War for Independence intensified in 1920, with the IRA conducting a series of ambushes and raids of police barracks, in a war of attrition that led to hundreds of British and IRA casualties. In that year alone, the IRA killed 165 members of the Royal Irish Constabulary. The situation in the North appeared starkest, with sectarian divisions again erupting in violence. Little helping matters was the passage on May 3 of the Government of Ireland Act placing Six Northern Counties— Antrim, Down, Armagh, Fermanagh, Derry, and Tyrone—under the control of a parliament based in Belfast, which in turn was tied to Westminster. This was a stunning blow to nationalists, who had long believed that Fermanagh and Tyrone would not be excluded from a southern republic. Others had not believed that partition would actually take place. However, the IPP's Joseph Devlin had warned that the establishment of a Northern government would amount to "permanent partition," while the party's MPs condemned the act as destined to "'stereotype racial and religious differences' by creating an 'artificial area' under the 'ascendancy party.'"[57] The Government of Ireland Act appeared to ensure that artificial barriers of a territorial, ethnic, and religious nature were being drawn.

One clause of that legislative measure called for the setting up of a Council of Ireland, which would seek to eventually unify the entire island under a single parliament. James Craig, who served as the first prime minister of Northern Ireland, responded that sympathetic treatment, but never coercion, might win over Ulster. Thomas Hennessey contends that Unionists readily admitted they were devising "an arbitrary border" inside Ireland to safeguard "their interests." However, "they did not accept that this diluted their claim that there should be a border in Ireland, for if nationalists wished to secede from the rest of the British Isles, then Unionists believed that they had a right to secede

In January 1921, Sir Greenwood inspects the paramilitary force called the Black and Tans that was employed to assist the Royal Irish Constabulary.

from the rest of Ireland."[58] Lines were being drawn that established arbitrary borders splintering Ireland.

One week following Unionist leader Edward Carson's delivery of an address to an Orange gathering on July 12, in which he asserted, "I am sick of words without action," Protestants rampaged through Catholic districts in Derry and Belfast.[59] With violence mounting, Sinn Féin and IRA supporters in the North initiated the Belfast Boycott Committee, which urged Dail Eireann to respond to the purported war of extermination being conducted against them. A paramilitary force called the *Black and Tans*, made up primarily of former British soldiers, was employed to assist the RIC, but became notorious because of brutal actions they committed. In October, Sir Ernest Clark, the Assistant Under-Secretary in the Irish Office in London, supported the formation of the Ulster Special Constabulary, which, by the end of 1920, amounted to over 20,000 men, to help rein

Treaty negotiations between the Sinn Féin and the British government led to the Anglo-Irish Treaty signed on December 6, 1921 by Michael Collins. From left to right: Irish nationalist leader and founder of Sinn Féin, Arthur Griffith; E.J. Duggan, Irish soldier; Minister for Defence, Michael Collins; Anglo-Irish politician and author Erskine Childerds; Gavin Duffy; R.C. Barton; and J. Charteris.

in Sinn Féin activity in Belfast. While Protestants viewed the Special Constabulary as necessary to stave off IRA terror, Catholics considered the "Specials" (as they were known) repressive agents. The violence continued unabated. On November 21, IRA fighters in Dublin murdered more than a dozen individuals, many of whom were involved with intelligence operations; that same day, two IRA men under arrest were killed while purportedly attempting an escape, and 12 other individuals were gunned down by British forces searching for IRA members.

In the midst of the fighting, elections were held for the Northern Ireland Parliament. Collins, who was leading the IRA's military operations in the South, supported Sinn Féin's participation in the elections, calling for successful nationalist candidates to join the Dail and boycott the Northern government.

Collins's support for absention from electoral campaigns was based on his desire to ensure the Irish people did not get accustomed to the idea of partition. De Valera favored absention to maintain unity for the Republic, while the IPP also opposed partition, deeming it both unnatural and antagonistic to Irish nationalism. Both De Valera and the IPP feared that partition would result in a carving up of Ireland, something they were determined to prevent.

On May 5, 1921, de Valera and James Craig met in Dublin, with no conclusive results, although the recently passed Government of Ireland Act was suspended temporarily. Elections that month resulted in a sweep for uncontested Sinn Féin candidates in the South, and victory by most Unionist candidates in Ulster; six Sinn Féin and six IPP candidates did prevail in Northern campaigns. The half-dozen Sinn Féin victors in Ulster proclaimed themselves bound for the Dail, not the Belfast parliament. Two months later, a truce was announced in Ireland, with de Valera and Craig traveling to London to talk with Lloyd George. Public statements made by those who had taken power in Northern Ireland, Cardinal Michael Logue of Armagh warned, suggested that Catholics might soon encounter persecution. In August 1921, loyalist paramilitary forces, such as the Ulster Protestant Volunteers, intensified their activities, carrying out assassinations of Catholics. While British soldiers intervened in the wake of rioting, additional violence led to the remobilization of the Specials in the early fall, but more disturbances occurred shortly thereafter.

In October, the Second Dail instructed a republican delegation—Collins and Griffith were among the members—to conduct negotiations with the British. On November 10, Lloyd George discussed the possibility of a united Ireland but encountered firm resistance from Ulster's James Craig. On December 5, de Valera indicated from Limerick that it was "for complete freedom ... they in Ireland were struggling." Pressured to sign the Anglo-Irish Treaty on December 6, Collins, who believed he had signed his own death warrant, and Griffith failed to consult with de Valera or the cabinet in Dublin, a decision that had pro-found implications for Irish republicans. The *Anglo-Irish Treaty* established an Irish Free State, made up of 26 of Ireland's coun-ties, which was to become a dominion within the British Commonwealth, but whose very existence ensured that partition and arbitrary borders were now formally in place. Provisions allowed Northern Ireland to opt out of the Irish Free State, for Article 12 required Northern Ireland's boundaries to be deter-mined "in accordance with the wishes of the inhabitants" and established a Boundary Commission.[60] The question arose, nev-ertheless, which counties would choose partition.

The Anglo-Irish Treaty seemingly ended the War for Independence, while establishing the Irish Free State. Yet the longstanding hopes of republicans remained unfulfilled, because the Treaty seemed to ensure the partition of Ireland and corre-sponding arbitrary borders, which they had so bitterly opposed. Republicans fought one another, due to differences regarding the treaty and the apparent recognition that Northern Ireland would remain a Protestant bastion, as least for the foreseeable future. Thus, Ireland soon endured another violent chasm, this one pitting nationalists against one another.

5

The Irish
Civil War

The apparent compromise resulting in the Anglo-Irish Treaty hardly satisfied everyone. The Speaker of the Dail, Eoin MacNeill, urged a policy of non-recognition through passive resistance. Readying to depart from the Dail, Minister of Defense Cathal Brugha declared:

> If ... our last cartridge had been spent and our last man was lying on the ground and his enemies howling round him and their bayonets raised, ready to plunge them into his body, that man should say ... if they said to him: "Now will you come into the Empire?" ... "No, I will not." That is the spirit which has lasted all through the centuries and you people in favour of the Treaty know that the British Government and the British Empire will have gone down before that spirit dies out in Ireland.[61]

The *Irish News,* linked to the Irish Parliamentary Party, praised the Treaty, declaring that "not since 1172 have the Irish masses been supreme in their own country for a single year." Now, the newspaper editorialized, "a measure of national liberty has been placed at the disposal of the 75 per cent of the Irish people who live in the 26 counties."[62] While admitting that the agreement was not "ideal," Arthur Griffith termed it "a Treaty of equality." He insisted, "We have brought back the flag; we have brought back the evacuation of Ireland after 700 years by British troops and the formation of an Irish army. We have brought back to Ireland her full rights and powers of fiscal control."[63]

The treaty, Lloyd George claimed, allowed for the creation of Northern Ireland, a prime example of artificially drawn boundaries. At the same time, he warned that if Ulster were to exist as "a separate community," only coercion would allow for the retention of Fermanagh and Tyrone. Charles Curtis Craig, brother of the Unionist leader, retorted that the loss of those counties would prove disastrous: "Our Northern area will be so cut up and mutilated that we shall no longer be masters in our own house."[64] Completing its debate on the treaty, the Dail approved of it by a narrow 64–57 vote on January 7, 1922.

Disputes regarding the Anglo-Irish Treaty continued to splinter the republican camp badly, eventually leading former comrades to war with one another. The scholar Richard English suggests that the issue of partition was not foremost on the minds of those who had previously fought together against British control. In the midst of negotiations prior to the vote in the Dail, even de Valera had offered the possibility of coupling acceptance of the Treaty with the Irish Republic's participation in the British Commonwealth. Still, many republicans did demand complete separation from British rule in any fashion. They failed to appreciate that compromise, which would amount to the acceptance of various arbitrary borders, appeared necessary to prevent the continuation of a bloody war with Britain.

The Civil War in Ireland, Brian Feeney also contends, did not result from partition, but rather involved the issue of "swearing allegiance to 'foreign kings' and whether that meant the Treaty had fatally compromised the ideal of the Republic."[65] Indeed, the British government had already carved out Northern Ireland as a distinct political entity, as exemplified by the parliament in Belfast and the Ulster Special Constabulary. Similar to the general membership, most of the leaders of Sinn Féin, including Collins and Griffith, supported the Treaty, but de Valera opposed it, leading to a division in the organization he still headed. Guiding the anti-Treaty forces, de Valera, backed by many activists and several Dail legislators, all of whom were tied to the IRA, insisted his opponents should depart from Sinn Féin.

As republican forces splintered into Treatyites and the anti-Treaty IRA, Specials and vigilante Loyalists undertook a murderous campaign against nationalist forces in Ulster. The British government struggled to set up a series of meetings between Collins and James Craig, the Unionist leader, to curb the violence in the North. Collins, already in the midst of a political battle with de Valera, struggled to convince nationalists in border areas that the Northern parliament would no longer remain in control of large sections of Armagh or places like Newry.

Meeting in London in late January and in Dublin in early February 1922, Collins and Craig discussed border concerns, with the IRA chieftain expressing his desire for half of Ulster.

MICHAEL COLLINS

Raised in West Cork, the heartland of the Fenians, Michael Collins (1890–1922) grew up hearing tales of Irish rebellion. His teacher, a Fenian, was also a member of the Irish Republican Brotherhood. As a child, Collins read nationalist newspapers and subscribed to the *United Irishman*, which Arthur Griffith, the founder of Sinn Féin, edited. In 1906, Collins served as a clerk at the West Kensington Post Office in London. He soon became a member of the Gaelic Athletic Association, the Gaelic League, and Sinn Féin; by 1909, he belonged to the IRB. After working for a number of companies, where he acquired financial expertise, Collins returned to Ireland, during a period when the movement for Home Rule was gaining support.

Arriving in Dublin in 1916, Collins, who had joined the Irish Volunteers, participated in the Easter Rising, but later became critical of the amateurish manner in which the rebellion was conducted. Collins, along with many other Volunteers, was shipped to England, where he was imprisoned before being placed in a camp in Wales. Released in late December, Collins became secretary of the Irish National Aid and Volunteer Dependants Fund. Attempting to

Michael Collins, Commander in Chief of the National Forces of the Irish Free State, poses in uniform on August 14, 1922. Collins was killed just eight days later during an ambush at Beal nam Blath while touring his home county of Cork.

Craig responded by stating that Protestant Unionists would never relinquish Londonderry and Enniskillen.

Shortly after the collapse of the talks, the IRA conducted

garner support for the Volunteers and the IRB, Collins also backed Sinn Féin's electoral campaigns, which sponsored a demand for release of 120 other prisoners, including Eamon de Valera and Thomas Ashe. Collins supported de Valera's election as president of Sinn Féin, which was urging recognition of an Irish republic. Heading an intelligence operation for Sinn Féin, Collins was imprisoned for speaking against conscription.

Let out on bail, he went underground, soon becoming president of The Organisation, as the IRB was now called. He oversaw an arms-smuggling operation and put together a squad of assassins called the Twelve Apostles. At the same time, Collins was instrumental in helping to ensure Sinn Féin's sweeping electoral triumph in 1918, but along with many other successful candidates, refused to take his seat in Westminster. Collins also failed to show up for the newly formed Irish parliament, the Dail Eireann, because he, along with another MP, was plotting de Valera's escape from Lincoln Prison. The newly reassembled Dail, meeting in April 1920, chose Collins as Minister of Finance. With de Valera in exile overseas, Collins and Cathal Brugha took control of the Irish Republic's war of terror against British rule. Relying on several members of the Irish Republican Army, drawn from the Volunteers, Collins, now the most wanted man in Ireland, established a new spy apparatus that carried out assassinations of British agents on the island. Nevertheless, he and Arthur Griffith went to London at de Valera's behest, for a series of peace talks that resulted in the Anglo-Irish Treaty in early December 1921.

The Anglo-Irish Treaty tore apart the republican movement, as it now divided into the Treatyites, who numbered Collins and Griffith among their ranks, and the anti-Treaty IRA, headed by de Valera. After the Dail Eireann ratified the Treaty, de Valera resigned as head of state, while Collins was named Chairman of the Provisional Government. Tensions built up and civil war erupted on June 28, 1921, when Collins ordered an attack on the headquarters of the anti-Treaty IRA, Dublin's Four Courts garrison. Less than two months later, assassins ambushed Collins, who as the national army's Commander-in-Chief was conducting a tour of inspection of his native Cork. Tens of thousands turned up in Dublin for his funeral procession.

In July 1922, additional violence broke out in Belfast. The Civil Authority Act passed that year enabled security forces to search homes without warrant and employ violence during interrogation of suspects.

several border raids, which resulted in the kidnapping of several Unionists. British officials heightened security measures in the North; a gun battle occurred between the IRA and members of the Ulster Special Constabulary, soon backed by the Royal Ulster Constabulary; loyalists pushed Catholics out of their home in Fermanagh; and additional violence broke out in Belfast. In May, the Northern Ireland government declared the IRA and its affiliate organizations illegal, and carried out the internment of those accused of terrorism. Eventually, hundreds were interned, resulting in the near-fatal crippling of Sinn Féin; by contrast, IRA leaders generally managed to avoid the latest dragnet. The Civil Authority or *Special Powers Act* of 1922 enabled security forces in the North to search homes without warrants, prevent meetings and rallies from being held, employ violence during interrogations of suspects, and carry out hangings. The IRA responded by attempting to wreak havoc within the Six Northern Counties, but its forces were severely outnumbered by the Specials.

Collins felt compelled to act, facing mounting criticism from de Valera regarding the violence confronting Northern Catholics. On May 18, pro- and anti-Treaty forces came together for a meeting, with Collins, Griffith, and de Valera all in attendance. The beleaguered Northerners insisted on "a united civil government supported by a united army," but the divisions between republicans remained in place.[66] Seeking to defend the Catholic population in Ulster, Collins helped to arm both Treatyites and anti-Treaty IRA in the North, which appeared to legitimize the taking up of arms against a duly constituted government.

Three days before new elections, scheduled for June 10, 1922, Collins sent two agents to assassinate Sir Henry Wilson, military adviser for the Belfast government, in front of the Englishman's home in London. Also on June 7, republican headquarters, based at the Four Courts garrison in Dublin, sponsored the kidnapping of General O'Connell, the Irish Free State's army chief of staff. On June 9, former British Secretary of War and Air Winston Churchill delivered an address in the House of Commons in which he warned that the British Empire could not allow for establishment of an Irish republic. The elections on June 10 failed to resolve the quandary, with pro-Treaty forces winning nearly three times as many seats in the new Dail as those who refused to swear allegiance to the British monarchy.

While Collins and Northern IRA officers soon decided to suspend military operations in the North, causing many Treatyites in that region to believe that the Dail had abandoned them, the differences separating former republican allies soon spawned a frenzy of violence. The fighting occurred within the 26 Counties of the Free State. On June 28, 1922, the army of the Free State directed artillery, obtained from the British, at the Four Courts garrison. The anti-Treaty IRA lacked good military leaders and faced determined Treatyites, guided by Collins, who could draw on support from London. Informing Collins that no compromise could take place, Churchill offered aircraft to bomb the republican forces into submission.

The Civil War took the lives of still more nationalists, on both sides of the latest Irish divide, which remained political, ideological, and territorial. In July 1922, Cathal Brugha was gunned down, leading a top IRA figure who supported the Treaty to declare his former comrade "a man of kindliest nature, a sincere friend, gentle in manner, but ... as firm as steel, and as brave as a lion." A mere ten days after the death of Arthur Griffith, who suffered a fatal cerebral hemorrhage, Michael Collins was assassinated by anti-Treaty IRA gunmen on August 22. Informed that Collins was conducting an inspection of Cork, his home county, gunmen ambushed him while he was traveling in an open touring car. Later, Liam Lynch, serving as the anti-Treaty IRA's chief of staff, was also murdered, leading a compatriot to produce a poem on his behalf:

> Dead comrade! You who were a living force
> Are now a battle cry, on our long roll....
> You, who in life,
> Have shown us how to live and now have
> Taught us how to die, teach us still....
> Courage and strength to further the cause
> Of our endeavor—a nation free.[67]

The Irish Free State government ordered the executions of 77 anti-Treaty IRA, many of which took place without any trial. At one point, the Dail considered asking if the British would ship prisoners to St. Helena, the infamous island prison that had once held Napoleon Bonaparte. Throughout the 10-month long civil war, the Free State imprisoned 12,000 Republicans. The anti-Treaty IRA murdered two Dail representatives on December 7, the day following official establishment of the Irish Free State. The very next day, to deliver a warning, the Treatyites killed four incarcerated anti-Treaty IRA members. The message was received, and the number of political assassinations diminished.

Even when the civil war ended in May 1923, many IRA republicans remained imprisoned. That led to a mass hunger strike, initiated in October, which involved thousands of prisoners demanding to be released from jail; the strike ended after several weeks, having failed to produce the desired results.

While the bloody civil war thus came to a close, left to be resolved were questions involving both Northern Ireland and the Irish Free State. Boundary disputes regarding arbitrary borders continued, along with the question of the status of Catholics in the North and of Protestants in the 26 Counties of the Free State. The Anglo-Irish Treaty and the civil war that followed ensured that partition and its artificial frontiers remained in place. However, many still favored the reunification of Northern Ireland and the Irish Free State and the island's emergence as a full-fledged republic, separate from Great Britain. Protestants in the North, many considering themselves more British than Irish, were wholly adverse to those very possibilities. Thus, the seeds for more tension and, hence, greater violence, were sown, allowing for additional discontent and threatening new eruptions.

6

Irish Statehood and the Six Northern Counties

The civil war helped to ensure that James Craig's government in Northern Ireland could quell the military threat posed by anti-partition forces. Even while the struggle in the South continued, the Free State sought to employ the Boundary Commission to bring about a united Ireland and terminate British-Unionist sponsored arbitrary borders. To the delight of the Dublin regime, the British General Election of December 1923 led to the formation of a Labour government headed by Ramsay MacDonald, although it lasted for only 10 months. However, Craig refused London's request that he select a representative for the Boundary Commission.

Despite persistent opposition from Unionists, the Commission finally met in early November 1924, a hopeful sign to the Catholic minority in Northern Ireland. The optimism proved misplaced, as suggested by an early determination by British officials to avoid the transference of large amounts of territory. In January 1925, Craig told the British government that he would not be able to disband the Specials until after delivery of the Commission's report. An election in April actually resulted in a victory by nationalists in Fermanagh and Tyrone counties, as well as in West Belfast and Derry. However, on December 3, the Free State representative agreed to accept the present boundary and to support the establishment of a Council of Ireland, which would supposedly bring about cooperation between the Dublin and Belfast governments. London promised to defend the existing frontiers. Thus, to the dismay of border nationalists and republicans supportive of Eamon de Valera, the Government of Ireland Act of 1920 continued to set the boundaries for Northern Ireland. Sinn Féin's Cahir Healy charged that border nationalists had been terribly betrayed.

Problems lay ahead for Northern Ireland, which took on the appearance of a Protestant state as arbitrarily drawn borders threatened to become permanent. As Richard English suggests, "The nationalist perception that the north was an illegitimate creation was lastingly retained by Northern Catholics; it was also, understandably, reinforced by the discriminatory unionist actions that it had helped to encourage."[68] All the while, the Free State was becoming more republicanized, producing a greater divide between the two bodies. In the North, Unionists deliberately sought to create a Protestant state controlled by the Orange movement; in the Free State, the Catholic nature of Irish society similarly intensified. The Belfast government deliberately chose to retain large numbers of security forces, along with a considerable amount of repressive legislation, to maintain control of Catholic nationalists. The Unionists also benefited from the abandonment of proportional representation, which during the 1920s temporarily enabled nationalists to control more local public bodies and elect a larger number of MPs. *Gerrymandering*, which involved the redrawing of electoral boundaries to benefit Unionists, worked to the disadvantage of nationalists and Labour Party candidates. Consequently, the Catholic minority considered itself disenfranchised and discriminated against.

All this proved troubling to many who continued to dream of a united Ireland. Five years after the end of the Civil War, a member of the IRA, which had suffered defeat in Northern Ireland and had splintered in the South, bemoaned the continued existence of the Belfast regime.

> Twelve years after Easter Week Ireland remains, unfree and unredeemed, still bound to the British empire .... It is twelve years since Clarke and Connolly and Pearse proclaimed the Irish republic. It is five years since the last shot was fired in its defense. Cowardice, treachery and war-weariness have prevailed; Ireland is again held in the British empire.[69]

In the Irish Free State, de Valera remained a dominant figure. Imprisoned by the Dublin government in August 1923, de Valera was one of 15,000 Sinn Féin and IRA prisoners released from internment camps by mid-July 1924. Many members of Sinn Féin, to which the IRA continued to pay allegiance, refused to accept the legitimacy of the Dublin parliament. Eventually, de Valera departed from Sinn Féin and in May 1926, he formed a new political party, *Fianna Fail*, whose title, "Soldiers of Destiny," had been taken from the Volunteers. The supporters of Fianna Fail considered themselves the only true Irish republicans, but abandoning the policy of absention, they began contesting elections within a year after the party's founding. In June 1927, Fianna Fail captured 44 seats to but 5 for Sinn Féin and only 3 seats less than the governing Cumann na nGaedheal, whose hard-line ideological perspective had politically crippled it. The IRA, which experienced a period when it was declared illegal, increasingly began to lend support to Fianna Fail.

De Valera and Fianna Fail took power in the Free State after the Great Depression (1929–1940) began ravaging Ireland, both South and North. The severity of the economic downturn threatened the Unionist hold on power in Northern Ireland, albeit only temporarily, in 1932. That same year, Fianna Fail acquired control of the Irish parliament in Dublin, leading to de Valera's selection as president of the Executive Committee. Economic difficulties long afflicted Northern Ireland, which had been saddled with high levels of unemployment when the Belfast government was established. In the mid-1920s, conditions in Belfast were so severe at one point that thousands suffered the possibility of starvation, and warnings were delivered that dire conditions could trigger a revolution. Not helping matters was a trade war with England that occurred after Fianna Fail became the governing party.

The worldwide depression that unfolded in the early 1930s crippled Northern Ireland, with unemployment approaching 30 percent, disastrously affecting both Protestants and Catholics. In 1932, at the height of the depression, Protestant and Catholic joined together to condemn reductions in the aid to the poor, as riots broke out in various British cities. Anger intensified, as indigent residents in Belfast, for example, became aware that they were receiving less than half of what those on relief did in Glasgow, Scotland. Mass gatherings and rallies protesting the severe economic circumstances took place, with the communist Revolutionary Workers' Groups (RWG) sometimes igniting the protests. The government banned a mass march scheduled for October 11, and the Royal Ulster Constabulary moved to prevent the rally, which the RWG remained determined to hold, from taking place. The RWG threatened a general strike, while hundreds of police poured into Belfast. Talking at St. Mary's Hall before a group of women and girls on October 10, the activist Tommy Geehan noted that "for many years the workers of Belfast had been divided by artificial barriers of religion and politics."

THE ROYAL ULSTER CONSTABULARY

Emerging out of the century-old Royal Irish Constabulary, which had moved against the Fenian Brotherhood and urban rioters, the Royal Ulster Constabulary (RUC) first appeared on June 1, 1922. Led by Inspector General Charles Wickham, the RUC carried arms and tackled the problem of sectarian disturbances and political assassinations in Belfast. Initially, the RUC was supposed to have a 3,000-man force, with a third of those positions slotted for Catholics. However, many nationalists urged fellow Catholics not to join the RUC, while the leaders of the police organization hardly favored hiring them. Particularly feared were the B Specials, Protestant police auxiliaries tied to the RUC, who greatly outnumbered the regular RUC forces; Sir Basil Brooke initially founded the B Specials in Brookeborough, calling on individuals who been involved with the Ulster Volunteers or served in the British army. Brooke, like the B Specials, considered Catholics suspect; he intended that the B Specials be employed to help solidify the arbitrary borders that separated Ulster from Southern Ireland. Repeatedly, the B Specials went after IRA members, often relying on the Special Powers Act, as the RUC in general did.

Not officially decommissioned, the RUC became less active by the end of the 1920s but was turned to again during the Great Depression because of labor unrest. Beginning with the outbreak of World War II, the RUC addressed smuggling operations from the 26 Counties of the Free State. All the while, Unionists viewed this police force favorably, considering it a bulwark of the Protestant-dominated government in Stormont. Nationalists encouraged their supporters not to join the RUC, which served as a symbol of heavy-handed domination by Ulster Protestants.

Now, those same workers appeared "united on a common plat-
form demanding the right to live."[70]

On October 11, rioting erupted in Protestant and Catholic
communities, with many injuries and a pair of deaths resulting.
A Labour Party secretary warned that British officials sought to
separate laborers into competing religious factions. Seeking to
blame republicans and communists for the unrest, a Unionist
leader reminded that there existed "Ulster forces able to deal
with these people ... who had had no love for the Union Jack."
James Craig, now Lord Craigavon, insisted that if troublemakers
considered "this ... one step toward securing a Republic for all
Ireland.... Then I say they are doomed to bitter disappoint-
ment."[71] Nevertheless, the Poor Law Guardians, who established
relief rates, increased those amounts, leading the RWG to claim
victory.

The Protestant-Catholic partnership proved short-lived, as
sectarianism soon reappeared in Northern Ireland. As Fianna
Fail swept to victory in the Free State's General Elections in 1932,
Northern nationalists watched expectantly, hoping to be welcomed into the Dail Eireann; to their chagrin, however, de Valera
turned down the request and offered no advice on a policy of
absention at Stormont. Fianna Fail's triumph troubled
Unionists, who worried that the Free State would undertake
incursions against the North, as had occurred in the years 1920
to 1922. The extremist Ulster Protestant League condemned the
recent labor unrest that had erupted in Northern Ireland and
began to amass considerable support from top Unionist Party
members.

Discussion took place regarding whether Catholics could
ever be loyal to the Northern government. Controversy swirled
as Sir Basil Brooke, who worked for the Unionist administration, informed an Orange audience that Loyalists should only
employ good Protestants. James McCarroll, a Nationalist Party
MP from Foyle, denied that "any man born in Ireland is a dis-
loyalist. I do not admit that any man born in Cork, Kerry, or
anywhere else in this country, is disloyal if he is loyal to his

native land." The sentiments expressed by Brooke, McCarroll charged, were targeted "not against ... mythical disloyalists ... from the Free State, but ... against the Catholic Irishmen bred and born in the Six Counties."[72] In 1932, anger regarding the Unionists' near-absolute hold on power led most Nationalist Party members of the Belfast Parliament to begin boycotting its proceedings. De Valera's governance certainly helped to shape the attitude of Northern nationalist politicians, with one abstaining MP acknowledging that he looked to the Free State leader for guidance.

Various sectarian disturbances occurred over the next years, but they heightened dramatically in 1935 as celebrations marking the 25th anniversary of the ascension of King George V (reign 1910–1936) approached. In July, Belfast experienced riots over the span of three weeks that left 13 dead, many injured, and hundreds, most of them Catholic, homeless. Unionists, Sir Brooke asserted, only opposed those Catholics who wanted to break away from the British Empire. Thus, this was not a religious fight, but rather a political one. The *Irish News*, a nationalist publication, acknowledged that Northern Catholics desired a United Ireland, but insisted that most sought to achieve that through constitutional means. Nationalists remained divided among themselves regarding absention.

The Irish Free State possessed concerns of its own, including political unrest that involved first the Blueshirts, a right-wing group evidently patterned after Italian fascists, and then the IRA. Both the IRA and Fianna Fail had employed vigilantism to harass Cumann na nGaedheal, which purportedly resulted in the emergence of the Blueshirt movement. In helping crush the Blueshirts, the already weakened IRA shifted further to the left, demonstrating a hard-line stance regarding constitutionalism. Following a pair of assassinations committed by IRA forces, de Valera's government acted in 1936 to temporarily outlaw the organization.

For their part, Northern Unionists unhappily tracked the course of events in the Free State, which continued to experience

In 1937, Eamon de Valera introduced a new Irish constitution that made Ireland a sovereign state and gave himself the title of Taoiseach, or prime minister. He was reelected to his position in 1948, 1951, and 1957. He is shown here in December 1937 on the steps of a government building in Dublin.

Gaeliciation (involving a greater emphasis on Irish nationalism), culminating in a new constitution adopted on July 2, 1937. Article 2 declared, "The national territory consists of the whole island of Ireland, its islands and the territorial seas." Article 3 indicated that,

> pending the re-integration of the national territory, and without prejudice to the right of the Parliament and Government established by this Constitution to exercise jurisdiction over the whole of that territory, the laws enacted by that Parliament shall have the like area and extent of application as the laws of Saorstat Eireann and the like extra-territorial effect.

Several provisions underscored the primacy of the Catholic

Church in Eire, as the Irish Free State was now renamed. Article 41 effectively made no provision for divorce, while article 44 affirmed that the Catholic Church held a "special position" in Eire's life.[73]

Northern nationalists applauded the new constitution, even though it apparently underscored that the government of Eire only held sway over the 26 Counties that had made up the Free State. Sinn Féin's Cahir Healy appeared pleased that the document at least acknowledged the existence of partition or arbitrary borders, which had been ignored in the Irish Free State's earlier constitution. Craigavon expressed no concerns about the new instrument, declaring that Northern Ireland's relation to the British Empire would not be affected by what transpired in Southern Ireland. Still, many Unionists continued to view Eire as a threat to the North.

To resolve longstanding disputes, including the trade war, British and Irish representatives gathered in the spring of 1938. Northern nationalists and Unionists viewed the announcement of such sessions quite differently. The *Irish News* hoped that partition might be abandoned, a possibility Ulster Unionists feared. While Craigavon insisted that Unionists would yield nothing, Northern Nationalists bemoaned the destruction of their Irish nationhood. Thus, "until we are united with our brethren of the rest of Ireland not only are we deprived of our rights as Irishmen but the historic Irish nation, unnaturally divisioned, is robbed of its glory and greatness." Northern nationalists looked to England to rectify the situation. As Cahir Healy noted, only England, which had created partition, could end it.

The outbreak of World War II dramatically affected Ireland, both North and South. The war compelled the governments in Belfast and Dublin to undertake strenuous efforts to stifle IRA activities, which included, by 1939, the planting of bombs in England and Northern Ireland. The IRA proclaimed, "England is the enemy of Ireland's freedom. The English have partitioned our country. They enforce partition by bayonets and are responsible for the persecution and victimization of Irish citizens in northeast Ulster."[74] After three IRA fighters died in late November 1938 while attempting to construct a bomb, the Royal Ulster Constabulary and the B Specials intensified their operations, and internment was initiated yet again. Demanding the removal of all British military units from Ireland, the IRA nevertheless set off bombs in England in mid-January 1939. An IRA manifesto of January 16 condemned partition, declaring that it continued "old English tactics of 'Divide and Conquer'," splitting Ireland "into two parts with two separate parliaments subject to and controlled by the British Government from London."[75] Thus, the IRA remained adamantly opposed to the presence of arbitrary borders that divided and allowed for English colonial rule. Over 100 explosions occurred by July, leading to passage of the Prevention of Violence Bill, which required the registration of Irish citizens residing in Britain and allowed for them to be deported. On August 25, a bomb killed 5 and wounded over 50 people at a shopping center in Coventry, further enraging the general English populace.

The outrage the bombings produced, the start of World War II, and de Valera's determination to reign in the IRA together effectively brought an end to the organization's bombing campaign in England. The Dublin government, led by de Valera, who had promised that Eire would not be employed as a base to attack Britain, relied on the Offences Against the State Act, passed in June, which allowed for internment. Only days later, the IRA was again outlawed, while in late August, a special military court was set up. An Emergency Powers Bill passed in early September. Although a high court tossed out the provision providing for internment, the IRA's capture of over a million rounds of Army ammunition in December led to the passage of the Emergency Powers (Amendment) Act, restoring the power of internment. Protesting de Valera's stance, nine IRA prisoners undertook a hunger strike, leading to the death of two men but no concessions. The IRA shifted its course, again targeting the North, where it conducted a series of bombing attacks in 1940. Drawing on the Special Powers Act, Stormont demanded that identity cards be held by everyone over the age of 14, and insisted that Southerners who crossed over the border prove their designs were peaceful. The repressive moves in both Eire and Northern Ireland all but crushed the IRA, which further wounded its reputation by reaching out to Nazi Germany; nevertheless, the IRA carried out a series of actions in the North, which invariably led to still harsher measures by the Belfast government.

While handling the threat posed by the IRA somewhat similarly, de Valera and Craigavon responded quite differently to Great Britain's participation in World War II, with Eire becoming the one dominion to remain neutral, a stance Northern nationalists approved of. To the dismay of Ulster Unionists, the British government, in June 1940, began negotiating with the Dublin regime about the possibility of Eire's abandoning neutrality if Great Britain indicated support for Irish unity. De Valera, however, failed to respond favorably to the proposal and Northern Ireland remained an integral part of the British war effort. Northern Ireland paid the price for such loyalty, suffering German bombings over a four-day period in Belfast alone that led to 1,100 deaths, 56,000 houses damaged, and 100,000 left temporarily homeless. Although Unionists wanted the British government to extend conscription to Northern Ireland, strong opposition, led by nationalists and the Catholic Church, convinced London that it would hardly be worth the trouble that would undoubtedly ensue. Eire's continued adherence to a policy of neutrality convinced British intelligence that de Valera had afforded the British citizenry a strong rationale to maintain partition.

World War II, Thomas Hennessey suggests, strengthened "the psychological gap between Ulster unionism and Irish nationalism," a chasm that would prove difficult to surmount. The Unionist Sir Basil Brooke, who became prime minister of Northern Ireland in 1943 (and became known as Lord Brookeborough), admitted that a lengthy "anti-British feeling" existed in the rest of Ireland. By contrast, he contended, "Here there is a pro-British feeling.... That is the boundary of the mind which exists between us and the south."[76]

Shortly following the end of the European theater of the war, the Labour Party won an overwhelming victory in the British General Elections, held in July 1945. As British Labour members had long bitterly criticized their government's policies in Northern Ireland, Northern nationalists now discarded absention, choosing instead to take their seats in both Westminster and Stormont. The *Irish News* suggested that Nationalist MPs could do "everything in their power to forward the claims of the Irish people for the unity and sovereignty of the Irish nation, unnaturally divided twenty years ago by the British government."[77] The election of a British Labour government greatly worried Northern Unionists, who distrusted Labour's socialist perspective and its critical stance regarding Northern Ireland. As matters turned out, Northern Ireland actually benefited from agreements made with the new British government to extend the welfare state to Ulster. The Catholic Church opposed welfare provisions, fearing their supposed authoritarian tendencies.

Opposition to partition continued, with a new organization, the Irish Anti-Partition League, appearing in late 1945. The weakening of Fianna Fail, due in part to the repression meted out during the war, actually provided impetus to Northern nationalists. Another new organization, Clann na Poblachta, began capturing Dail seats by late 1947 and soon agreed to join a coalition government that included the Southern Labour Party and the Fine Gael party (previously known as Cumann na nGaedheal), which had become associated with the Blueshirts. In 1948, that government took over from de Valera, who had presided over the Irish Free State or Eire for the past 16 years. Fine Gael's John A. Costello received the title of *Taoiseach*, or prime minister, and declared on September 7 that Eire would become a republic and leave the British Commonwealth. Both Unionists and Northern nationalists believed that this would lead to a general campaign to terminate partition.

For over a quarter-century, the 26 Counties of the Irish Free State or Eire, in line with the 1920 Government of Ireland Act and the Anglo-Irish Treaty of December 1922, had been partitioned from the Six Northern Counties. Eamon de Valera had been the single most important figure in the development of the Free State or Eire, while engaging in a balancing act concerning partition. De Valera had been on the losing side of the Irish Civil War, and joined with those republicans who insisted on a full Irish state and who refused to accept the compromise Arthur Griffith and Michael Collins had agreed to with British negotiators. Recognizing the futility of a dogmatic anti-partition stance, however, de Valera broke from Sinn Féin and established Fianna Fail, which became first the leading oppositional force and then the governing party in the Irish Free State or Eire. While continuing to indicate his belief in a unified Irish nation, de Valera, increasingly the realist, clamped down on IRA intransigents who demanded the creation of a republic made up of all of Ireland's 32 counties. De Valera maintained Eire's neutral stance during World War II, but Dublin's repressive approach diminished his appeal and that of Fianna Fail, leading to its eventual electoral defeat. Ironically, that paved the way for a new government determined to carve out an Irish republic, albeit within 26 Counties alone. Consequently, the arbitrary borders, devised two decades earlier and separating Northern Ireland and the Irish Free State or Eire, threatened to become permanent.

7

Border Conflicts

The Irish Labour Party (ILP), meeting shortly after Taoiseach Costello's announcement that Eire would soon become the Republic of Ireland, declared itself to be made up of "unrepentant anti-partitionists." Throughout England, the Republic of Ireland, and Northern Ireland, Labour Party activists remained determined to "get rid of the border and have a united Ireland."[78] The ILP thus demanded an end to the artificial frontiers that splintered Ireland, a division that continued to disturb or even enrage most Irish nationalists. However, opposition arose to the ILP's seemingly intransigent position, resulting in the emergence of a Northern branch of the party, which supported the existing constitutional framework including partition and Ulster's position inside the Commonwealth. Author and political activist Conor Cruise O'Brien, who belonged to the ILP, warned that Unionists must be convinced that the collapse of borders would not lead to Catholic oppression of Protestants.

De Valera appeared no happier in the South, and his party boycotted the official proclamation of April 18, 1949, declaring Ireland a republic and announcing its withdrawal from the British Commonwealth. Fianna Fail refused to attend the ceremony, with de Valera insisting that his party demanded a republic in all of Ireland, including the Six Northern Counties. On June 2, 1949, the Ireland Bill, intended to define relations between Great Britain and the Irish republic, became law. Parliament affirmed that Northern Ireland remained tied to the United Kingdom, a relationship that would not end without the approval of the Belfast government. Many Northern nationalists proved dissatisfied, unsuccessfully turning to the Anti-Partition League to have absentionists admitted to the Dail.

Mounting frustration eventually enabled the IRA to regain a certain footing. In 1949, a Sinn Féin vice-president, Christoir O'Neill, declared that "the aim of the Army is simply to drive the invader from the soil of Ireland and to restore the sovereign independent Republic proclaimed in 1916." Thus, the IRA intended to conduct "a successful military campaign against the

British forces of occupation in the Six Counties." As Sinn Féin increasingly came under the sway of the IRA, the political organization adopted a similar agenda. Its new constitution in late 1951 also proclaimed that the Irish people owed allegiance to the Irish Republic, as it had been declared 35 years earlier. Also, in 1951, the IRA conducted the first of a series of major raids against military bases in Northern Ireland. In the raid against the Ebrington Barracks in Derry, the IRA grabbed a series of weapons, along with ammunition. After an IRA member was sentenced for his role in another raid, which was carried out in mid-1953 against the Felstead School Officers' Training Corps in Essex, he defiantly refused to apologize. Cathal Goulding asserted, "We believe that the only way to drive the British Army from our country is by force of arms, for that purpose we think it no crime to capture arms from our enemies."[79] Splinter groups conducted raids of their own.

The attacks frightened Unionists, who strengthened the Royal Ulster Constabulary commando units and placed 200 B Specials on full-time duty. Stormont went further, relying on the Special Powers Act to ban various groups, including Sinn Féin, which in 1955 had garnered the largest vote total signifying opposition to partition that any organization had received in over three decades. In effect, this seemingly ensured that republicans possessed no peaceful means of expressing their viewpoints in an organized fashion. Undoubtedly, that convinced the IRA to kick off Operation Harvest, a plan of guerrilla warfare five years in the making, which involved border raids first undertaken in the early morning of December 12, 1956. The IRA announced its goal: "an independent, united, democratic Irish republic. For this we shall fight until the invader is driven from our soil and victory is ours."[80] Four IRA units, containing approximately 120 men, split into smaller contingents and went after various targets across Ulster. Sinn Féin announced that Irish citizens were again combating British aggression in their homeland. British Prime Minister Anthony Eden indicated that Westminster would ensure security for Northern Ireland.

Stormont itself responded by again reverting to internment without trial, but the number of attacks increased—over 500 were eventually carried out—notwithstanding the absence of support from nationalists in the North or from the general public in the Republic of Ireland. The government in Dublin fell in early 1957, replaced by Fianna Fail and Eamon de Valera, back in power for yet another stint as head of the 26 Counties. Once again, like the Unionists in the north, de Valera did not hesitate to clamp down on the IRA and reintroduce internment. De Valera's successor, Sean Lemass, proved no more sympathetic to the border raiders. Operation Harvest dissipated, and on February 26, 1962, the IRA declared that it was terminating "The Campaign of Resistance to British Occupation." The IRA acknowledged that the public had "been deliberately distracted from the supreme issue facing the Irish people—the unity and freedom of Ireland."[81] The *New York Times* applauded the announcement that the border wars had ended.

> The original I.R.A. and Sinn Féin came in like lions ... and now they go out like lambs ... the Irish Republican Army belongs to history, and it belongs to better men in times that are gone. So does the Sinn Féin. Let us put a wreath of red roses on their grave and move on.[82]

Throughout the period of the border wars, partition continued to hold the attention of leading political figures in the Republic of Ireland, Northern Ireland, and England. On October 15, 1959, Taoiseach Sean Lemass, during an Oxford Union debate on the subject, declared support for "the growth of a practical system of co-operation between the two areas even in advance of any political arrangement." Lemass asked if it did not make sense, regardless of one's positions on "the eventual reunification of Ireland ... that the two existing communities in our small island should seek every opportunity of working together in practical matters for their mutual and common good?" Continuing, he warned against expecting quick results, for "the barriers of fear and suspicion in the minds of partitionists are too strong to be demolished quickly." Yet he expressed his belief that the most significant obstacles to reunification were internally drawn and that Westminster "could and should undo its historic responsibility for partition by declaring that it would like to see partition ended 'by agreement among the Irish.'"[83] The question remained, however, whether that would suffice, given the opposition of Unionists.

Nevertheless, change was in the offing, as suggested by the resignation on March 23, 1963, of Viscount Brookeborough, as prime minister of Northern Ireland. It had been Brookeborough who had rebuilt the Ulster Volunteer Force and created the B Specials over four decades earlier. Craigavon had wanted Brookeborough to succeed him, and after the short-lived tenure of J.M. Andrews, he had done exactly that. Brookeborough had remained determined to crush any threat emanating from the IRA and had viewed Ulster as a wholly distinct community from the Irish Republic. As his tenure in office continued, however, Brookeborough's governance appeared steadily more complacent. Not helping matters was the rise in unemployment to 9.5 percent of the workforce. Thus, many welcomed the announcement that Brookeborough would be replaced as the leader of Northern Ireland by Captain Terrence O'Neill, who had served as his Minister of Finance.

Throughout this period, Unionist forces in Ulster scarcely demonstrated any conciliatory determinations toward the Catholic minority; nationalist forces sometimes responded in kind. Back in 1954, the Belfast government passed the Flags and Emblems (Display) Act, which supported the flying of the Union Jack. Those who sought public employment had to take an oath of allegiance to the British monarch. Nationalists often preferred to play "Amhran na bhFiann," the national anthem of the Republic of Ireland, and refused to stand when "God Save the Queen" was aired. Few intermarriages occurred, while almost all Catholic children enrolled in *parochial schools*, educational institutions that their church ran. Top government officials referred to Catholics as "traitors" and decried "appeasement" in their own midst.[84] The holding of Orange parades proved highly unsettling to Catholic communities, which led to economic boycotts and riots at various points. Most Unionists expressed disinterest in accepting Catholics into the Unionist Party. Catholics largely dwelled in all-Catholic districts, which were often viewed as *ghettoes*, sections of a city where people are forced to live because of social, economic, or legal pressure. A number of Catholics did establish National Unity, which hoped to reform the Nationalist Party by championing a united Ireland, condemning violence, and urging acceptance of the existing Northern constitution.

As matters turned out, the sectarian divide helped to ensure that Northern Ireland remained a somewhat tenuous affair, even though the IRA appeared to have been vanquished. Through 1962, when the IRA's Campaign of Resistance ended, republicans had long been associated with violent efforts to eradicate English control. For decades, Protestants, beginning with Wolfe Tone in the late eighteenth century, had joined in such drives, sometimes leading them. Along the way, military might, repression, and economic destitution had crippled republican efforts, with many subdued, incarcerated, or driven into exile. All the while, Irish history appeared to center around resistance to English rule, which resulted in "a splendid chronicle of heroes and martyrs and villains."[85] Irish republicans emphasized the continued resistance, rather than the defeats that piled up. Through the Easter Rising of 1916, both Protestants and Catholics joined in insurrectionary activity at various points, as they would again in the war against English dominance that occurred through 1922. Increasingly, as had been true by the end of the nineteenth century, Catholics disproportionately made up the ranks of the agitators, revolutionaries, and fighters determined to create an Irish republic. Indeed, sectarian divisions were heightened by the Easter Rising and the ensuing guerrilla war waged by Irish revolutionaries against the British. More and more, IRA recruits, almost without exception, were Catholic. The establishment of Northern Ireland only furthered this development, while republicans divided into various factions. Those divisions continued, despite the end of the Irish Civil War, the establishment of the Irish Free State, and the setting up of an Irish republic in the 26 Counties. Moreover, arbitrary territorial borders intensified religious fissures.

By the early 1960s, two Irelands existed, as did a pair of Northern Irelands, as author J. Bowyer Bell suggests. The Republic of Ireland remained largely rural, parochial, and religious, with the Catholic Church battling against cultural changes that appeared more and more inevitable. Taoiseach Lemass, however, desired change, prosperity, and modernity, supporting a pair of economic expansion programs, which required increased external trade. Automobiles and new mechanical devices became more commonplace, along with improved medical care, educational facilities, and a transformed middle class that appeared more cosmopolitan. Cultural conservatism failed to abate entirely, with censors continuing to examine books and films, divorce all-but-impossible to obtain, and abortion illegal. Moreover, greater change occurred in urban areas like Dublin, which sheltered nearly a fourth of the Republic's 2.8 million people, than in rural pockets spread across the Southern landscape.

In Northern Ireland, religiosity also prevailed and characterized Catholics and various kinds of Protestants. Indeed, divisions marked the Six Northern Counties, including the sectarian and political split that separated pro-British Protestants, who happily waved the British flag, and Catholics, who remained nationalists, almost without exception. Protestant children attended public schools, where they learned British history, while Catholic children went to parochial schools, where they played Gaelic games and received a distinctly different version of historical events, both ancient and of more recent vintage. Protestants in the North appeared even more religious and loyal to the British crown than did their badly outnumbered counterparts in the Republic; Catholics in Ulster believed that eventually territorial barriers would end. As Bell writes, "In time partition would be undone, the island united, a nation once again; justice would be done, history redeemed and fulfilled." Consequently, the two groups had different heroes, different traditions, and a different reading of history. But while Catholics in Northern Ireland looked to Dublin for guidance, most inhabitants of the Republic considered them "as parochial and irrelevant as the loyalists were to London."[86]

In the Six Northern Counties, Protestants and Catholics wrestled with tensions that always lay just beneath the surface. Insults were frequently delivered or experienced, even when they were not intentionally offered. Many believed that separation remained Northern Ireland's best hope, the one possibility for retaining even a semblance of civility. Thus, as Bell notes,

> Neighborhoods were segregated. Businesses, clubs, pubs, games, churches, hospitals, schools, all the institutions and arenas of society existed for either tradition but rarely for both. Big stores and central cinemas catered to money, but elsewhere there were Catholic pubs and Protestant tailors, deep in areas of their own. In small towns, in the mixed countryside, in the border neighborhoods, a constant, never-ending dance of delicate adjustment took place so that offense need not be given nor intimacy encourage.[87]

Sparks, in the form of deliberately devised rallies and marches, could easily trigger explosions. Protestants intentionally coursed their Orange parades, complete with political statements, through Catholic districts. Catholics responded in kind, with fiery nationalists and republicans displaying the flag of the Republic of Ireland to commemorate days sacred to republicanism. The Royal Ulster Constabulary was seemingly ever-present at public ceremonies, as were hints that IRA would resurface yet again. Somehow, this not always delicate dance continued, decade after decade.

For Protestants, their continued, near-monopolistic hold on power required not only continued British support but also a demographic advantage allowing them to control local councils and Stormont. British backing, depending on whether Conservative or Labour governments were in power, was not always perfectly reliable. And even though Protestants remained the majority religious group in Northern Ireland, that was not true in Ulster's western provinces or in places like West Belfast and Derry. Even the arbitrary borders intended to solidify Protestant control increasingly appeared unlikely to retain that dominance, given demographic changes and cultural transformations that were occurring. This necessitated other actions on the part of Protestant leaders, ranging from reform efforts to police campaigns designed to thwart Catholic nationalism.

8

Efforts
at Reform

The new prime minister of Northern Ireland, Terence O'Neill, possessed an ambitious agenda for the Six Northern Counties. To diminish the growing attraction of the Northern Ireland Labour Party (NLIP) for Protestant workers, O'Neill employed a technocratic approach to modernize the province's economy; he induced several leading manufacturers, including Michelin, Goodyear, and Du Pont, to establish branches in Northern Ireland. At the same time, O'Neill hoped that improved economic conditions would also appeal to Catholics and dampen the sectarian nature of Ulster politics. As he indicated, "I have been trying ... to persuade Catholics in Northern Ireland that they have a place within the United Kingdom."[88] O'Neill refuted the notion that segregation resulted from deliberate policies, arguing instead that Protestants and Catholics voluntarily set themselves apart from each another, a contention that contained grains of truth but hardly excused discriminatory practices. In June 1963, O'Neill offered condolences following the death of Pope John XXIII, while the next year, he delivered an important gesture by visiting a Catholic school. None of this pleased Unionist hard-liners, who had favored the election of Brian Faulkner as head of state.

In addition, the prime minister exchanged peace feelers with the Irish Republic, while affirming that "the fundamental purpose of Unionism ... is to preserve a parliamentary union with Great Britain" that dated back to the beginning of the nineteenth century. Indeed, as North-South relations improved, the Nationalist Party agreed to become, for the initial time, the official opposition in the Belfast parliament. In Dublin, Taoiseach Sean Lemass actually little identified with Northern nationalism, considering both it and the Belfast government conservative and sectarian. The Taoiseach's government even dismissed charges of discrimination experienced by Ulster Catholics, with one senior official acknowledging that "it was regrettable but true that very little, if any interest in the problems of the Northern Ireland minority is taken outside Ireland."[89]

In reality, Catholics had experienced some gains during the

previous two decades. Thanks to greater educational opportuni-
ties and economic transformations, a larger number of
Catholics fit within the ranks of the middle class. However,
public employment remained largely off limits, so Catholics
established various organizations demanding greater equity.
These included the Campaign for Social Justice (CSJ), which
appeared in May 1963 because of frustration regarding the
seemingly impotent nature of Nationalist Party representatives
in Stormont. Within a short while, the CSJ began insisting that
the British government pay greater attention to discriminatory
developments in Northern Ireland.

Hopes for a more enlightened policy arose when Great
Britain's General Elections in 1964 brought Harold Wilson and
the Labour party to power, but the new British prime minister
proved reluctant to act. Intensified pressure would force Wilson
to do so, particularly after the Campaign for Democracy in
Ulster (CDU) appeared in mid-1965. Backed by more than 100
Labour MPs and lords, the CDU called for an inquiry to explore
government practices in Northern Ireland, with a particular
focus on housing, employment, political boundaries, public
appointments, and religious discrimination. It also appeared
noteworthy that the West Belfast district elected Gerry Fitt, an
Irish Labour member, to Parliament. Nevertheless, Wilson preferred behind-the-scenes talks with O'Neill, whom he viewed as
a legitimate reformer confronting threats from Northern
nationalists adverse to changes in policies favoring Protestants.

O'Neill, unlike his predecessor, also proved willing to establish better relations with the Republic of Ireland. In mid-January
1965, Taoiseach Lemass traveled to Belfast to talk with O'Neill at
Stormont, the first session between the leaders of the two
Irelands in four decades. They delivered a brief announcement,
expressing a willingness to examine further what cooperative
endeavors might be possible. The next month, O'Neill went to
Dublin for another encounter with Lemass, and a series of meetings between various government ministers followed. That May,
O'Neill and Harold Wilson spoke in London, and the British

prime minister indicated strong support for the North-South discussions. The talks proved disconcerting to various members of the Unionist Party, who roundly denounced O'Neill for exchanging visits with Lemass without consulting the Northern Ireland cabinet and prior to the Irish Republic's recognition of the Belfast government.

Most troubling to O'Neill, perhaps, was the greater publicity being garnered by the Reverend Ian Paisley, an extreme Unionist who, back in 1951, had established his own Free Presbyterian Church, which was virulently anti-Catholic. Later that decade, Paisley helped to form Ulster Protestant Action, which called for preferential treatment of Protestant laborers during hard economic times, something Northern Ireland frequently experienced. Paisley's support proved instrumental in the election of a pair of rabid Unionists, Desmond Boal and John McQuade. Then, in September 1964, the Royal Ulster Constabulary acceded to Paisley's threat by removing the flag of the Irish Republic from Sinn Féin election headquarters in West Belfast. The worst riots since the mid-1930s unfolded in Belfast, with fears developing that the government might have to request Army troops.

Once the violence subsided, Paisley continued to attack O'Neill, putting out the *Protestant Telegraph*, a weekly newspaper that stridently attacked both Catholics and communists. Paisley's hatred of Catholicism was virtually unbounded. He charged that "Priestcraft, superstition and papalism with all their attendant voices of murder, theft, immorality, lust and incest blocked the way to the land of gospel liberty." In April 1966, he convinced the Belfast government to call on the B Specials, as well as to ban trains crossing the border from the Irish Republic, prior to celebrations honoring the 50th anniversary of the Easter Rising. After Paisley was convicted on July 18 of both instigating a riot in a Catholic district of Belfast and goading his followers to attack government officials, his supporters exploded in rage, battling the RUC. Paisley's loyalty to the Northern Ireland government was clearly conditional, as when he warned, "If the Crown in Parliament decreed to put Ulster into a United Ireland, we would be disloyal to her Majesty if we did not resist such a surrender to her enemies."[90]

In the first half of 1966, other disturbing incidents occurred in Northern Ireland, including petrol attacks (gasoline fire-bombs) directed against Catholic stores, houses, and schools, as well as the shooting of a number of Catholics. In May, the Ulster Volunteer Force (UVF), supposedly derived from the earlier group but actually made up of Paisley supporters, declared "war against the IRA, and its splinter groups" and promised that "known IRA men will be executed mercilessly and without hesitation."[91] Increasingly, denouncements of O'Neill and other government ministers could be heard at Orange rallies.

Another threat to O'Neill's governance emanated from still-disaffected Catholics, who were distressed that he failed to end political gerrymandering, general discrimination, or the presence of the B Specials. Moreover, some of O'Neill's economic reforms actually heightened economic disparities between Northern Ireland's geographic sectors, with the Catholic majority in the West and South experiencing higher levels of unemployment than the strongly Protestant East and North. Derry, with its Catholic majority, appeared particularly crippled, with nearly one out of every five of its male workers jobless. There, less than 20 percent of municipal positions were held by Catholics. Over 20,000 Catholics acquired only eight city councilors, while 10,000 Protestants elected a dozen. In County Fermanagh, which also possessed more Catholics than Protestants, twice as many houses built in the postwar period were allocated to Protestants. Rail closings also dramatically affected Derry and Fermanagh county.

Thus, four years into the O'Neill reform administration, Northern Ireland, as Marcus Tanner offers, "remained a Protestant state, run by a Protestant parliament, guarded by a Protestant police force." Earlier, a group of Labour MPs had demanded an inquiry into government operations in Northern Ireland. A schoolteacher in Derry, which Tanner terms "the eye of the coming storm," suggested that O'Neill "speaks reason, appeals for moderation and does nothing."[92] Catholics, for their part, appeared to be lacking both representation and political leadership. However, the IRA had apparently been mortally wounded by its failed border campaign, while Sinn Féin seemed to suffer from irrelevance. All of that would soon change, as a civil rights movement began to emerge in Northern Ireland.

The Wolfe Tone Societies, through which intellectuals and militant republicans discussed public issues, and the Campaign for Social Justice proved instrumental in the establishment on January 29, 1967, of the Northern Ireland Civil Rights Association (NICRA). The NICRA's constitution insisted on protection of individual rights and attention being drawn to abuses of power. The NICRA also demanded that both the Special Powers Act and the B Specials be abolished. The new organization urged support for the principle of "One Man, One Vote" and a cessation of gerrymandering. In October, the IRA's Roy Johnson called for a civil rights movement that would attract both Catholics and Protestants, but no such development took place.

The NICRA began conducting public marches and rallies, leading to one of the most important early developments in the course of the Irish civil rights struggle. The NICRA scheduled a rally for Derry on October 5, 1968, although many local Nationalists refused to participate in the march, slated to head into the heart of the city, ringed with a wall representing Protestant dominance. Although the NICRA appeared ready to cancel the march, more radical elements insisted it proceed, despite an edict from William Craig, Northern Ireland's Minister for Home Affairs, who refused to allow the procession to move outside the Catholic district. Nevertheless, 2,000 marchers appeared, soon confronting RUC units and a pair of water cannons. As a government report later acknowledged, the police got out-of-hand, pummeling the marchers. Fighting spread across Derry, which experienced its first gasoline firebombs, and barricades soon shielded the Bogside. Angered Nationalist Party members refused to continue as the official opposition in Stormont and British Prime Minister Harold Wilson soon demanded reforms in Northern Ireland. The Irish Republic's new Taoiseach, Jack Lynch, complained to Wilson about events in the Six Northern Counties.

On November 16, Derry experienced a 15,000-person march led by the Citizens' Action Committee, a moderate group headed by John Hume and Ivan Cooper, which confronted a vast array of RUC forces. Day after day, Derry laborers violated Craig's edicts, passing through the city's walled section, until O'Neill declared a series of reforms. While that angered Unionists, it in no way satisfied the civil rights activists, who demanded "One Man, One Vote," and an end to gerrymandering, something O'Neill could not agree to without tearing the Unionist Party apart. Minister of Home Affairs Craig warned that his Unionist Party would fight every attempt to pull its members into a United Irish Republic. Another march—this time sanctioned— began on November 30 but ran up against an illegal counter-demonstration led by Ian Paisley. The RUC seemingly sided with Paisley's group but prevented the civil rights marchers from leaving the Catholic ghetto. On December 9, O'Neill spoke before television cameras, indicating how he had striven throughout his tenure to bridge chasms between Protestants and Catholics.

Additional demonstrations and counter-rallies continued until early January 1969, when the RUC evidently allowed Loyalist thugs to batter civil rights marchers just outside of Derry. O'Neill's intemperate speech afterward, which blamed the civil rights force and threatened the employment of the B Specials, hardly helped to diminish tensions. Despite his heated rhetoric, O'Neill received harsh criticism from within the ranks of the Unionist Party. Clashes also occurred between civil rights activists and Northern nationalists; in a by-election, the NICRA's John Hume defeated Nationalist Party leader Eddie McAteer. On April 17, Bernadette Devlin, a member of the radical People's Democracy, won a seat at Westminster. Within two days, a riot began in central Derry, intensifying before the RUC swept into the Bogside. Derry threatened to erupt until the RUC forces were withdrawn. Protests led to riots throughout much of Northern Ireland, with Belfast experiencing the first overt moves by the IRA, which amounted to a number of bombings, since the civil rights movement had begun.

When additional rioting broke out, O'Neill responded by announcing support for the idea of "One Man, One Vote." However, only days later, O'Neill, following the bombing of water pipelines feeding into Belfast, felt compelled to resign from his post. In a television address, O'Neill defended himself: "I have tried to break the chains of ancient hatreds." Then, in inflammatory words, he talked about the need to provide Catholics with good jobs and homes so they would not "have eighteen children" and dwell "in the most ghastly hovel," relying "on National Assistance." O'Neill concluded, "If you treat Roman Catholics with due consideration and kindness, they will live like Protestants, in spite of the authoritative nature of their Church." [93]

O'Neill's replacement by Major James Chichester-Clark failed to address the continued perception that Catholics were oppressed or to alter the unwillingness of many Unionists to accept any change regarding their preferential status. New clashes soon ensued, resulting from Orange parades in places like Derry, rioting involving the Bogside, the banning of a People's Democracy march, and an eruption by Loyalists. All this led to the infamous events of August 1969, when a march by thousands of Orangemen produced another explosion in the Bogside.

Turning to armored cars to knock down barricades closing off the Bogside, the RUC also employed CS gas for the initial time in Northern Ireland. As rumors mounted, the Irish Republic's prime minister, Jack Lynch, warned that the sending of British soldiers to Ulster would not be acceptable. Only a unified Ireland could address the problems in Northern Ireland, Lynch reflected. Still, authors David McKittrick and

In August 13, 1969, a policeman in riot gear fires tear gas at Catholic and Protestant rioters in the Bogside neighborhood, a Catholic area in Londonderry.

David McVea suggest that although Lynch wanted to demonstrate sympathy for Northern nationalists, he sought to prevent the Irish Republic from becoming directly ensnared in the Northern Troubles. Nevertheless, from this point forth, the Irish Republic was again embroiled in the Northern Ireland's problems.

By August 14, British troops arrived, a sight initially welcomed by Bogsiders, who soon came to view them in a different light. At this stage, the British cabinet remained opposed to the idea of direct rule, fearing that the British Army would necessarily confront republicans and Catholics in Northern Ireland. As top cabinet ministers acknowledged, they had to operate "through the Protestant Government. The Protestants are the majority and we can't afford to alienate them as well as the Catholics and find ourselves ruling Northern Ireland directly as a colony. We have also to be on the side of the Catholic minority and try to help and protect them against their persecutors."[94]

Harold Wilson's administration had undertaken a momentous leap in committing British soldiers to Northern Ireland, the price of retaining the region's arbitrary borders. Terence O'Neill's halting efforts at reform had only further inflamed an already volatile situation. Members of his own Unionist Party and other Ulster Protestants were at first frustrated, then enraged by O'Neill's conciliatory gestures toward the Catholic minority. Extremist forces, including those represented by the Reverend Ian Paisley, acquired a greater following as groups like the UVF and other Loyalists eagerly sought to battle against nationalists they considered too aggressive. Catholics split among themselves, with new organizations springing up due to frustrations about the obviously failed nature of previous responses by the nationalist community. Those organizations, and especially the most militant among them, proved determined to challenge the artificial barriers that had continuously relegated Catholics to an inferior position in the Six Northern Counties. As rallies and demonstrations surged forth, only to encounter security forces and vigilantes alike, the Catholic community of the Bogside turned to physical barricades of its own, trying to keep out both the RUC and Loyalist thugs. At the same time, their opponents remained determined to employ arbitrary borders to hold Catholics inside the Bogside, both physically and otherwise.

9

The Latest
British Takeover

On August 19, 1969, the British cabinet issued the Downing Street Declaration, which affirmed that Northern Ireland would remain tied to the United Kingdom unless the people of the Six Northern Counties opted for another solution. The statement pointedly indicated, "The border is not an issue," and also applauded the reforms the Belfast government had undertaken to ensure equal treatment for the residents of Northern Ireland.[95] The following day, British Prime Minister Harold Wilson promised the eventual disbandment of the B Specials, the establishment of a committee to consider reorganizing the Royal Ulster Constabulary, and the setting up a tribunal to explore the roots of the recent riots. The British Home Secretary, James Callahan, conducted walking tours through riot-torn sections of Belfast and Derry, to the delight of Catholics, and announced the release of men recently interned. As Callahan saw matters, the British government had deployed troops because of Stormont's failings.

The Declaration and the British government's subsequent actions hardly assuaged concerns in either the Unionist or the Catholic camp, while demonstrating the precarious nature of arbitrarily devised borders. The existence of No-Go areas, located behind barricades in Catholic districts, enraged Loyalists. With military or security areas unable to move into those spots, it seemed to Loyalists that portions of Northern Ireland had all but seceded. Loyalists battled with British soldiers, demanding that Catholic barricades be removed; recurrently, Loyalist riots broke out. Loyalists were no more enthralled when the Cameron Commission affirmed on September 12 that Catholics had suffered legal and political discrimination, and that the RUC and B Specials had engaged in illegal acts.

Displeasing too was the decision by Callahan to have the Army construct its "own barricade along the principal frontline between the two communities so that all the other barricades could come down automatically. This became the so-called peace line."[96] Nor were Loyalists happy that the Hunt Report, delivered on October 12, called for the RUC to be disarmed and the B Specials disbanded. Gun battles erupted, leading to the deaths of an RUC constable and two Protestants. Within a week, Thomas McDowell, who belonged to Paisley's church and the UVF, blew himself up while attempting to place a bomb at an electrical plant in County Donegal. Another bomb raced through the Wolfe Tone monument in County Kildare, and a third bomb hit the O'Connell monument in the middle of Dublin. Charges were brought against those—all connected to Paisley—who had ignited the explosions that doomed O'Neill.

The *Civil Rights News Service Bulletin* indicated that while the border was not in question, the existence of Stormont was. Republicans and the People's Democracy warned that British soldiers would soon target those who opposed the Belfast regime. Worry about that very possibility helped bring greater public attention to the IRA, which had quietly been supporting the civil rights movement. Even many old IRA fighters had considered their organization all but dead as the Troubles intensified. The IRA had been torn by sectarian divisions, with many disturbed by the left-wing position the organization adopted following the failed border campaign. As tensions heightened in Northern Ireland during the summer of 1969, the IRA hoped, to little avail, that Protestants would support the civil rights struggle. Disturbing also to IRA men was the graffiti on Belfast walls during the August disturbances that read, "IRA—I Ran Away."[97]

By the end of the year, the IRA had splintered. A militant group that called itself the *Provisional IRA* and another referred to as the *Provisional Sinn Féin,* many of whose families had long been involved with the organization and had experienced internment themselves, determined that military action was necessary. The Marxist-driven *Official IRA* and the *Official Sinn Féin* opposed that stance. Headed by individuals such as Sean Mac Stiofain, Ruairi O Bradaigh, and Daithi O Conaill, the Provisionals believed they were filling a void, in offering to provide protection for Catholic communities in Northern Ireland.

At the same time, the Provisionals remained determined to

remove the British from the North. Seeking an alliance with other radical forces, the Provisionals called for a national liberation front, and urged an end to the policy of absention. Their struggle, the Provisionals agreed, involved support for a 32-county republic, which had been betrayed because of the partition of Ireland that had occurred nearly half-a-century previously. In need of arms, they soon acquired a steady supply of guns, smuggled in from the United States. The Provisionals hoped to convince the British that Northern Ireland was ungovernable, which would result in the withdrawal of all troops. Seeking to strike at the "British occupation system" and its arbitrary borders, the Provisionals believed that "the illegal partition of Ireland" would lead to a military showdown.[98]

The Provisionals' prediction would be borne out as the upcoming decade proved to be the most violent Northern Ireland experienced in the twentieth century as efforts to shatter or retain the area's arbitrary borders repeatedly occurred. Responding to pressure from London, Chichester-Clark attempted to carry out additional reforms, which only angered hard-line Unionists. More violence unfolded, while Ian Paisley won a seat first in Stormont and then in the British Parliament. Moderates increasingly appeared outnumbered, despite the formation of the Alliance Party and the Social Democratic and Labour Party (SDLP). Moderate, non-sectarian Unionists founded the Alliance Party, while nationalists like Gerry Fitt, Paddy Devlin, and John Hume headed the SDLP, which effectively replaced the Nationalist Party and came to serve as a voice for the Northern Catholic middle class. Hume admitted that

> to many Irish Unity has come to mean the conquest of one state by the other rather than a partnership of both where both traditions combine in agreement to create a new society in Ireland, a pluralist society where all traditions are cherished and flourish equally....The border in Ireland is the psychological barrier between the two sections of the community in the North built on prejudice, sectarianism and fear.[99]

However, as working class Catholics came to view the British Army with hostility, the IRA garnered greater support as it intensified its campaign of guerrilla warfare. In October 1970, the IRA initiated a bombing campaign in Northern Ireland, generally targeting commercial centers. On February 6, 1971, Ensign Robert Harris became the first British soldier to die from the recent conflict, shot down by a member of the Provisionals' feared Third Battalion. Speaking on television the following day, Chichester-Clark declared that Northern Ireland was warring with the IRA Provisionals. Over the course of the next several months, the IRA and the British Army engaged in a deadly battle involving violence and reprisals. Chichester-Clark sought 3,000 additional troops, but after receiving less than half that number, which increased the total to 9,700, he resigned, with the Unionist Party selecting Brian Faulkner to replace him. Viewed as a hard-liner, Faulkner was associated with earlier internment efforts and believed that the Army could handle Northern Ireland. In early August 1971, thousands of Army and security forces began Operation Demetrius, which resulted in the rounding up of over 300 suspects. Charges of abusive treatment of those arrested soon followed. Internment without trial proved to be both a political and a military debacle, enraging the Catholic community, since only Catholics were picked up, and resulting in an escalation of IRA tactics. The IRA plotted to shoot security forces, policemen, and members of the Ulster Defence Regiment; to bomb economically sensitive spots; and to employ propaganda and intelligence gathering. Recognizing the futility of internment, loyalists determined to strike back on their own, also resorting to bombings and other vigilante actions.

By the close of 1971, 9 members of the IRA were dead, along with 33 Catholic civilians and 56 members of the security forces. IRA chortled that "England is on her knees; Stormont is finished" and proclaimed that the Six Northern Counties were "slipping from (the) grip" of the British.[100] At the same time, the Provisionals had recently made an effort to assuage certain concerns experienced by Protestants, talking about the need for four regional parliaments in Ireland, including the Dail Uladh (Ulster Dail). However, more Protestants joined the Ulster Defense Association (UDA), various paramilitary groups, or the new Democratic Unionist Party, which drew support from Paisley's followers.

On January 30, the event known as Bloody Sunday, which began as an anti-internment rally, unfolded in Derry, further enraging the Catholic community, already infuriated by the city's arbitrary borders. Referring to the Bogside, John Hume warned, "Many people down there feel now that it is a united Ireland or nothing." The Republic's Foreign Minister, Patrick Hillery, indicated, "From now on my aim is to get Britain out of Ireland."[101] Taoiseach Jack Lynch, who had been prodding London to add Catholics to the Northern Ireland government, referred to Bloody Sunday as "unbelievably savage and inhumane." The *Derry Journal* warned that anger against British soldiers was escalating to an unprecedented level. Despite such rhetoric, Protestant vigilantes quickened the pace of their operations, which William Craig seemingly applauded. At one in a series of massive rallies he led, Craig declared, "We must build up dossiers on those men and women in this country who are a menace to this country because one of these days, if and when the politicians fail us, it may be our job to liquidate the enemy."[102]

The British government under Conservative Party leader Edward Heath proceeded on March 24 to establish *direct rule* over Northern Ireland, closing Stormont. The level of violence only worsened, undoubtedly because of how the Provisionals and Loyalist paramilitary viewed the British takeover. The Provisionals believed that their actions had produced the ouster of the Unionist government, which in turn suggested that Britain's determination to hold onto Northern Ireland was flagging. Loyalists considered the demise of Stormont to be the result of Britain's unwillingness to unleash security forces and crush the IRA.

Now, the Provisionals and Protestant militia forces discarded many of the existing restraints. The Provisionals attacked off-duty

RUC officers and members of the Ulster Defense Regiment (UDR), set off car bombs, and employed snipers to shoot British troops. Angry Protestants resorted to vigilantism, with death squads appearing, including John White's notorious Shankill Road gang in Belfast. The purpose of groups like his, White acknowledged, was "to terrorize the terrorist. It was one community attacking another."[103] The British government finally responded by rounding up some loyalists, although the total of Protestant internees never came close to equaling the number of Catholics suffering internment. Protestant paramilitaries, including White's thugs, continued their operations, moving on to target nationalist politicians for assassination. By the end of 1972, that epochal year of the Troubles, nearly 500 people had been killed, ten times that number had been injured, and almost 2,000 bombings had taken place.

The British government established the Northern Ireland Office, headed by William Whitelaw, who sought to reach out to both Unionist and nationalist forces. Attempting to demonstrate good faith, Whitelaw released several internees and quelled a hunger strike, according republican prisoners special category status. The Northern Ireland Secretary also invited republican leaders, including both Gerry Adams and Martin McGuinness, to engage in secret talks at his home in Chelsea. News of this development appalled Unionists, who feared that Britain might be moving to withdraw from Northern Ireland. But after a brief IRA ceasefire ended, violence flared up yet again. In late 1972, Whitelaw eventually responded with the release of *The Future of Northern Ireland*, a document affirming the importance of power sharing and the need for the Republic of Ireland to help determine the future of Northern Ireland. Although the IRA believed such proposals only demonstrated the weakness of the British position, both the SLDP and Dublin welcomed Whitelaw's suggestions. However, few Unionist leaders did. Both the IRA and the Loyalists continued to strike at one another, with the Provisionals acquiring more sophisticated weapons from Libya, courtesy of Colonel Muammar al-Qaddafi.

London devised plans to establish a new assembly in Northern Ireland, where power sharing would be featured. In early December 1973, Unionist, SDLP, and Alliance delegates met, along with representatives from London and Dublin; this was the first such meeting involving the governments of the two Irelands and Great Britain since the mid-1920s. The resulting Sunningdale Agreement set up a Council of Ireland, called for security cooperation between the Republic and Northern Ireland, and sought to explore the constitutional makeup of the Six Northern Counties. Again, the Agreement proved troubling to Unionists, who worried about the Irish Republic's involvement in the affairs of Northern Ireland. The government in Dublin delivered a statement indicating that only a decision by the majority of inhabitants in Ulster could produce a change in Northern Ireland's status.

Brian Faulkner and Gerry Fitt headed the newly established Northern Ireland Executive, which had to contend with opposition from both Unionist hard-liners and the IRA. The Provisionals announced, "We look forward with confidence to 1974 as a year in which the British rule in Ireland shall be destroyed and the curse of alien power banished from our land for all time."[104] The Provisionals carried out a series of bombings, with one involving a motorcoach transporting British soldiers, which resulted in 12 deaths, including those of three civilians. Unionists, who refused to support the Sunningdale Agreement, threatened a general strike, causing Faulkner to resign from the Unionist Party. Loyalists were further distressed when Harold Wilson again returned to serve as British prime minister, replacing the Conservative leader, Edward Heath. Loyalists were more pleased when elections in March resulted in a near-sweep for Unionists opposed to Sunningdale. A Protestant labor strike in May crippled the Northern economy, while in the Irish Republic, bombings in Dublin and Monaghan killed 32 people. Loyalists claimed that the UVF carried out the strikes, although allegations later emerged that British intelligence was involved in the operations. The strike led to Faulkner's resignation and the end of an early power-sharing effort. Anarchy threatened to prevail in Northern Ireland. Frustrated by the turn of events, Hume began a lengthy quest to find a solution to Northern Ireland's troubles outside its borders, reaching out to London, Dublin, and the United States.

The new Northern Ireland Secretary, Merlyn Rees, declared both Sinn Féin and the UVF legal, and attempted to speak with representatives from those organizations. Such discussions did convince the Provisionals, who had been crippled by internments and the deaths of many republicans, to declare a halt to the fighting at different points in both 1974 and 1975, although bombing campaigns took place in between the ceasefires. In February, the Provisionals announced that they would adhere to a ceasefire indefinitely. Increasingly, the Provisionals directed their firepower at Protestants, not at British or security forces. Rees, in turn, released various internees, reduced the pace of military activities in Catholic districts, and established "incident centers" where republicans could express grievances. At the same time, the Secretary let it be known that Britain possessed no designs on Northern Ireland, desiring only to honor its promises to the people there. The British government's dealings with the IRA and Sinn Féin disturbed both the SDLP and Dublin.

Although the Provisionals generally adhered to the ceasefire, Loyalist vigilantes continued their attacks, leading the Provisionals to strike back, resulting in scores of killings. By late 1975, Rees announced that internment had ended, but he also informed Parliament that over 1,000 individuals had been charged with politically motivated acts of violence. Another fight unfolded between the Provisionals and the Official IRA, costing 11 lives. In 1976, the conflict led a pair of Catholic women from Belfast, Mairead Corrigan and Betty Williams, to initiate Community of Peace People, a grassroots movement of both Roman Catholic and Protestant citizens dedicated to ending the conflict in Northern Ireland. For their efforts, they were awarded the 1976 Nobel Peace Prize. The following year, as author Jack Holland indicated, would prove to be the conflict's

Separating the Catholic and the Protestant communities of Belfast, Northern Ireland, the "Peace Line" is a fifteen-foot-high wall that snakes its way for over 6 miles through the city.

turning point. The number of killings dropped sharply, while security forces slackened the pace of their operations. Fewer clashes occurred that pitted the Provisionals against British soldiers, and No-Go areas, other than perhaps in south Armagh, disappeared. Nevertheless, the army's undercover Special Air Services (SAS) unit continued its campaign of covert operations against the Provisionals, while Loyalist-conducted murders diminished markedly. The Royal Ulster Constabulary, calling on intelligence from the military, police forces, and the British MI5, acquired informers within the ranks of the IRA.

Arbitrary borders remained in place, as Jack Holland notes: "The Peace Line had become a wall fifteen feet high, dissecting west Belfast, a crude expression of the segregation that sectarian violence had imposed on the city."[105] Increasingly, leading members of the Provisional IRA determined that political engagement by Sinn Féin was necessary, along with continuation of the IRA's military operations. A pair of younger leaders, Gerry

Adams and Martin McGuinness, eventually came to replace older southerners like Ruairi O Bradaigh and Daithi O Conaill. The Provisionals decided to create a new IRA, which would be based on cells of small numbers of individuals, to be placed under an intelligence officer's command. The Provisionals focused more on hitting soft targets in rural Northern counties, employing women to set off firebombs in stores, movie theaters, hotels, and offices. Both the British and the Provisionals seemed to be engaged in a new war of attrition. On August 27, 1979, the Provisionals assassinated Earl Louis Mountbatten, the cousin of Queen Elizabeth II and a war hero, while he was vacationed in the Irish Republic; that same day, the Provisionals bombed a British military convoy situated along Northern Ireland's border, killing 18 soldiers, all but two of whom were members of the despised Parachute Regiment republicans blamed for Bloody Sunday. The Provisionals continued to accept the analysis delivered in the IRA Green Book, the original instruction manual for volunteers of the IRA, which insisted that "the nationhood of all Ireland has been an accepted fact for more than 1,500 years and has been recognized internationally as well." The invasion by the Normans was said to have initiated over "8 centuries of RELENTLESS AND UNREMITTING WARFARE," with the British ushering in "economic exploitation with the unjustly partitioned 6 counties remaining Britain's directly controlled old-style colony" and the Republic still in thrall to London.[106]

It was hardly surprising then that the British government, now headed by the decidedly conservative prime minister, Margaret Thatcher, adopted a rigid stance regarding IRA prisoners. This occurred in the very same period when the UDA began targeting top nationalist and republican politicians, with Bernadette Devlin McAliskey barely escaping assassination at one point. Frustration built among republican prisoners, many housed at the Maze, formerly known as Long Kesh prison. Beginning in late 1980, prisoners initiated a hunger strike. This was the latest in a series of tactics employed by prisoners to convince British officials to restore the special category status for political prisoners. Under special category status, political prisoners were housed in separate wings, allowed to wear their own clothes, and receive more visitors. Such status had ended in early 1976, leading prisoners to initiate the H-Blocks campaign by refusing to wear prison clothes and wrapping themselves in blankets instead. Visitations stopped and prison sentences lengthened, but a growing number of prisoners protested, with many pointing to the beatings they suffered and the fact that 19 prisoners had been murdered during the past five years. Hundreds resorted to being "on the blanket," but prison officials refused to budge. Lacking little support outside the republican movement, prisoners engaged in a "no wash" drive, which garnered considerable publicity.[107] Then in October 1980, prisoners began refusing to eat.

After one prisoner went blind, the strike was called off but another hunger strike—opposed by republicans on the outside—began on March 1, 1981, led by Bobby Sands, a member of the Provisional IRA. While the strike continued, Sands, who was facing a 14-year prison sentence for a weapons violation, ran with Sinn Féin's backing as the lone nationalist candidate for Fermanagh-South Tyrone, narrowly winning a seat in Westminster. However, on May 5, Sands died, providing another martyr for the republican cause. Some 100,000 people showed up for his funeral, and worldwide condemnations of Thatcher resulted. The prime minister responded by stating, "Mr. Sands was a convicted criminal. He chose to take his own life. It was a choice that his organisation did not allow to many of its victims."[108] By August, 10 strikers—seven IRA men and three from the Irish National Liberation Army—had died. Pressured by family members, the prisoners finally halted the hunger strike, having won no concessions. Nevertheless, shortly thereafter, the republican prisoners were allowed to wear their own clothing and other minor demands were met.

Over a 12-year span of time, Britain had attempted through various means to halt the Troubles in Northern Ireland. That effort had proved futile, as British soldiers, intelligence operatives, and government officials failed to diminish the anger and frustration besetting Northern Catholics. Indeed, British plans to reduce tensions involved the setting up of more artificial barriers that only further enraged the Catholic community. Moreover, the introduction of British soldiers led to the revitalization of the IRA, which in turn eventually caused a rebirth of the IRA's political wing, Sinn Féin. A dozen years into the period of heightened British involvement had in no way diminished the Troubles in the Six Northern Counties, which continued to be divided by religion and by nationalist sentiments.

10

More Hard Times and Good Friday

The Republican movement now opted for a twin-fold strategy for winning control of Northern Ireland: fielding Sinn Féin political candidates and continuing a military campaign, amounting to a war of attrition by the Provisional IRA against British occupation. Sinn Féin appeared particularly strong in Belfast, where the Social Democratic and Labor Party (SDLP), headed by John Hume since 1979, lagged behind. In 1983, Gerry Adams, who had earlier been distrustful of electoral politics, defeated Gerry Fitt to become an MP from West Belfast. That September, the Provisionals broke 38 of their members out of the Maze prison, most of whom were saddled with life sentences resulting from capital offenses. The newly elected president of Sinn Féin, Gerry Adams, declared, "Armed struggle is a necessary and morally correct form of resistance in the six counties against a government whose presence is rejected by the vast majority of Irish people."[109] In October 1984, the Provisionals struck at Prime Minister Thatcher, particularly despised because of her intransigent attitude toward the hunger strikers, narrowly failing to assassinate her and several members of the British cabinet who were attending a Conservative Party conference in Brighton. In 1984, Unionists attempted to assassinate Sein Féin's leader, Gerry Adams, seriously wounding him in Belfast.

Throughout this period, Hume continued his painstaking efforts to discover a peaceful solution for the Troubles in Northern Ireland. Garrett FitzGerald, the Irish Republic's Taoiseach, supported Hume's proposal for constitutional nationalist parties throughout Ireland to come to an agreement regarding Northern Ireland; FitzGerald also responded favorably because of his concerns about the growing political threat posed by Sinn Féin. Thus, in 1983 FitzGerald helped to create the New Ireland Forum, which contained delegates from the SDLP, Fianna Fail, the Irish Labour Party, and Fine Gael. The Forum declared that Irish nationalism was rooted in opposition to British control, but also demanded an overcoming of religious differences and a reaching out to Unionists, who clearly wanted to retain British ties. While indicating respect for that determination, the Forum called for "political arrangements for a new and sovereign Ireland ... to be freely negotiated and agreed to by the people of the North and the people of the South." Other proposed models included a two-province state and joint rule, shared by Britain and Ireland. Thatcher summarily rejected all three solutions, with a response referred to as "Out, out, out."[110] The Forum warned that constitutional politics were on trial.

Despite the temporary setback, the efforts of Hume and FitzGerald bore fruit in mid-November 1985, when the Anglo-Irish Agreement was signed, which also hearkened back to earlier efforts at cooperation by Thatcher and the Irish Republic. Discussion was heard that "the real border ... was not geographical but in men's minds," a highly astute analysis, given the Northern Ireland's stormy history.[111] To the dismay of Unionists, the agreement set up an Inter-Governmental Conference to grapple with political, security, and legal concerns. Article 1 affirmed "that any change in the status of Northern Ireland would only come about with the consent of a majority of the people of Northern Ireland."[112] Unionists condemned the Anglo-Irish Agreement, with James Molyneaux, who headed the Unionist Ulster Party, warning that under its terms Northern Ireland would be passed on from one country to another. His organization linked up with the Democratic Unionist Party (DUP), led by Ian Paisley, and conducted political boycotts, resulting in a new round of elections that increased the Loyalist vote.

Unionist violence also began to intensify yet again, as did that associated with the Provisionals, now buttressed by more weapons and explosives shipped from Libya; indeed, a leading government official in the Irish Republic suggested that the IRA's actions imperiled the state's very existence. The Provisionals attacked barracks, in an effort to set up liberated areas along the border with the Irish Republic. The British struck back, calling more frequently on the Special Air Services (SAS), commandos with orders to shoot to kill when necessary. On May 8, 1987, the SAS killed eight Provisionals, including four high-ranking members, when they attempted to strike at the Loughall RUC station in County Armagh. In October, French officials intercepted the ship *Eksund*, which was carrying a large shipment of weapons from Libya. The Provisionals suffered another kind of setback in November with the horrifying Enniskillen bombing, in which an IRA bomb left 11 dead and over 60 wounded, all of them civilians who had gathered for Memorial Day observances.

Sinn Féin's leader, Gerry Adams, had recently declared armed struggle to remain of the largest importance. Nevertheless, Adams called for the IRA to acknowledge that absention was outmoded. The IRA agreed, although a small group walked away to form Republican Sinn Féin and soon established a new Army Council, despite stark threats from their former compatriots. Adams's own organization began indicating that armed struggle was a political option. One reason for the shift in policy was the growing recognition that British forces continued to produce IRA casualties and capture IRA weapons, while the Provisionals' inability to avoid killing civilians proved politically crippling. Sinn Féin spoke of the need to equate opposition to British dominance of Ireland with an insistence on autonomy for the Irish people. Such a demand, Sinn Féin declared, would attain fruition "when the will of the British government to remain in Ireland will be eroded." Sinn Féin began conducting talks with the SDLP, but those discussions ended in the midst of another spate of violence, involving the killing of British soldiers and the shooting of IRA men. Adams considered the meeting with the SDLP to have been productive. There emerged "the shared political view that the Irish people as a whole have the right to national self-determination" and the sensibility that partition should be replaced by "constitutional, financial and political arrangements" to safeguard the rights of Ulster Protestants.[113]

However, the steady murder of soldiers convinced Prime Minister Thatcher to adopt a series of repressive measures, such as the banning of Sinn Féin from radio and television broadcasts and the loss of rights for those accused or convicted of paramilitary offenses. The Provisionals maintained their operations,

GERRY ADAMS

Born on October 6, 1948, in Ballymurphy, a working-class sector of West Belfast, Gerry Adams grew up in a staunchly republican household that was bitterly opposed to the arbitrary borders dividing Ireland. His father, also called Gerry Adams, was jailed in 1942 for having shot a member of the Royal Ulster Constabulary. The senior Adams belonged to the IRA, which for a time was headed by his brother Dominic. After completing his formal education, the younger Gerry Adams, already a member of the Belfast IRA, worked as a bartender and participated in the civil rights movement surfacing in Northern Ireland during the 1960s. Adams, whose mother also had distinguished republican roots with her brother an important IRA figure in his own right, quickly moved up the ranks of the Provisional IRA. In 1972, Adams suffered internment on a British prison, the Maidstone, where conditions were particularly harsh. After his release, Adams, although still only 24, was among the members of an IRA delegation that went to London for peace talks to grapple with problems resulting from Northern Ireland's arbitrary borders. The next year, however, he was again detained and held in prison for four years, without trial.

While incarcerated, Adams determined that military action alone would not allow republicans to prevail in their quest to terminate Northern Ireland's arbitrary borders. In 1977, Adams began serving on the IRA Army Council; the next year, he became vice-president of Sinn Féin. Adams was named president of Sinn Féin in 1983, the same year he was elected to Parliament from West Belfast, but he refused to occupy his seat because of the requirement that MPs take oaths of allegiance to the British crown. At the same time, Adams was working to convince Sinn Féin leaders about the need to participate more directly in Northern Ireland's political affairs. Behind the scenes, Adams began holding discussions with John Hume of the Social Democratic and Labour Party, a move that became instrumental in the peace process. Along the way, Adams began undertaking trips to the United States, where he was well-received, thus enabling Sinn Féin to obtain a higher profile. Through it all, Adams remained a controversial figure, condemned for regularly showing up at the funerals of IRA men and of helping to improve the image of the republican movement, in spite of the continued violence that Northern Ireland endured.

killing high-ranking RUC officers in early 1989, while in late September, they set off a bomb that murdered 11 soldiers in Deal, County Kent, in England. The Provisionals also attempted to assassinate Elizabeth II and several members of her family in mid-1990, by way of a food supervisor long connected to the IRA. After the bomb was discovered, the Provisionals devised a new tactic, the so-called human bomb, compelling a man from Derry to drive a stolen vehicle to a border checkpoint, where a device was set off, killing five soldiers.

At the same time, the British government, now headed by John Major, another Conservative leader, conducted secret negotiations with Sinn Féin's Martin McGuinness; these talks were later considered part of the peace process. Earlier attempts had taken place during the cease-fires of the mid-70s and again during the hunger strikes of the early 80s. In late January 1991, Gerry Adams insisted that "where you have an occupation force, Sinn Féin believes ... that people have the right to engage in armed resistance." Still, he prophetically declared, "The nineties is the decade in which peace can be agreed and we can start building a future."[114] The next year, Sinn Féin again called for partition to end but also asked for national reconciliation. However, on the very day, April 10, 1992, that Adams temporarily lost his MP seat in a general election, the Provisionals exploded two massive bombs in the City of London's financial district, producing damage estimated at over 750 million pounds, in addition to killing three people. In spite of the IRA-induced violence, four months later the British government banned the UDA, which was deemed responsible for having murdered approximately 500 people.

The action against the Loyalist organization was possibly a demonstration of good faith on Major's part, in the very period when his representatives continued to work with Sinn Féin to broker a peace deal of some sort. To the dismay of Unionists, the SDLP's John Hume called for both the Irish Republic and European states to become more involved in resolving the quandary of Northern Ireland. By late December 1992, the

Secretary of State for Northern Ireland, Patrick Mayhew, emphasized that Britain would respect the Protestant majority's desire for steadfast ties to the United Kingdom; he acknowledged an equally legitimate aspiration: the desire for a unified Ireland.

Word soon got out that Gerry Adams and John Hume were talking once again. On December 15, 1993, the British and Irish Republican governments, working off a draft by Hume, produced the Downing Street Declaration. Seeking to appease both nationalists and unionists, that document declared, "The British government agree that it is for the people of the island of Ireland alone, by agreement between the two parts respectively, to exercise their right of self-determination on the basis of consent, freely and concurrently given, north and south, to bring about a united Ireland, if that is their wish."[115] British Prime Minister Major promised to heed the wishes of the majority of people living in the Six Northern Counties whether they wanted to remain tied to Great Britain or become part of "sovereign united Ireland." The Republic of Ireland's leader, Albert Reynolds, stated that "it would be wrong to attempt to impose a united Ireland," without such a "freely" exercised desire on the part of Northern Ireland's inhabitants. Irish republican prisoners, situated in the infamous H-Blocks, indicated unhappiness with the Declaration, contending "that it ignores why partition has failed to bring peace, justice or stability to the people of this island.... It ignores Britain's responsibility and role."[116] Sinn Féin expressed its own displeasure with the agreement but continued to participate in the peace process, while Adams, in early 1994, undertook the first of a series of generally well-received visits to the United States, with his visa approved by the Clinton administration. Indeed, U.S. President Bill Clinton increasingly sought to become involved in the peace process, which proved unsettling to Prime Minister Major. In March, the Provisionals fired mortars at Heathrow Airport runways, while in June, UVF men committed a bloody rampage at a Catholic bar in Loughinisland in County Down, killing six.

As matters turned out, the level of violence soon diminished markedly. On August 31, 1994, the Provisionals announced that "in order to enhance the democratic peace process and underline our definitive commitment to its success," their leaders were proclaiming "a complete cessation of military operations." By mid-October, the Loyalist paramilitaries responded to this unilateral action, calling a halt to "all operations hostilities." Still, the British government insisted that Sinn Féin must guarantee a "permanent" peace.[117] Staunch loyalists soon created new political organizations, including the Progressive Unionist Party, but Ian Paisley attacked the peace process. In February 1995, Britain and the Irish Republic issued the Framework Document, which supported the continuance of the Union until the majority of people in Northern Ireland chose otherwise. It also called for greater involvement by the Irish Republic, by way of cross-border entities. While most nationalists welcomed the Document, most Unionists remained adverse to it. Still, Adams soon affirmed, "We subscribe to the classic, democratic position of Irish nationalism: Britain's partitioning of Ireland turned the Irish unionist minority into an artificial majority in the Six-County area."[118] Thus, as Adams saw matters, artificial borders could become permanently entrenched.

With negotiations expected to begin, an area of concern arose that threatened to derail the peace process: the weaponry at the disposal of the IRA. Pressure mounted for the IRA to relinquish those arms, but both the organization and Sinn Féin refused to accept that precondition. In November, London and Dublin agreed to support the establishment of a three-person commission, headed by former United States Senator George Mitchell, to examine the issue of IRA weapons. President Clinton visited Belfast and Derry that month, greeted enthusiastically by huge crowds as he spoke of the need for violence to end. In January, Mitchell's committee urged that decommissioning occur at the same time political negotiations took place. Sinn Féin insisted that British interference produced political strife in Ireland. Bombings soon occurred once more, although Ulster remained generally unscathed. However, the IRA was increasingly crippled by British intelligence operatives. In addition, Unionists, after rioting, defiantly marched along the Catholic Garvaghy Road in Portadown. A top security officer acknowledged, "We were on the brink of all-out civil war." He continued, "We kid ourselves that we live in a democracy. We have the potential in this community to have a Bosnia-style situation," alluding to the terrible cycle of violence afflicting the former Yugoslavia.[119]

Despite the increased violence and tension, the peace process went on, its prospects for peace apparently heightened by the Labour Party's easy triumph in the 1997 General Elections, which resulted in the prime ministership of Tony Blair. The total number of votes garnered by SDLP and Sinn Féin jumped considerably, with Sinn Féin's Martin McGuinness elected an MP and the Unionists losing control of four councils in Northern Ireland, including Belfast's. Blair welcomed Sinn Féin's participation in the peace process, to be chaired by Senator Mitchell. On July 20, the IRA affirmed that it remained committed to forcing the British out of Ireland. Nevertheless, the organization announced the restoration of a ceasefire. On September 10, Blair met face-to-face with Gerry Adams, the first time since 1921 that a British prime minister had spoken directly with a Sinn Féin leader. David Trimble of the Ulster Union Party also agreed to participate in the peace talks.

Although small paramilitary organizations and episodes of violence threatened to block the peace process, it continued, thanks to the determination of many of the key participants, including Blair, Adams, Hume, Trimble, and John Bruton, Taoiseach of the Irish Republic. Helpful too were Senator Mitchell and President Clinton; Mitchell later claimed that no peace agreement would have been possible without Bill Clinton. On April 10, 1998, the negotiating parties crafted the *Good Friday Agreement* (also known as the Belfast Agreement), calling for the residents of Northern Ireland to determine if it should remain with the Union or join the Irish Republic. Consequently, the Agreement required revisions of Articles 2 and 3 of the Irish constitution regarding a territorial claim to Northern Ireland. Considerable devolution (turning over) of power to a new Belfast assembly was to occur, although London still directed security matters. The new government would require support from both Unionist and nationalists, with a Unionist to serve as First Minister and a nationalist as Deputy First Minister. A British-Irish council would be set up, containing delegates from England, the Irish Republic, Scotland, Wales, and Northern Ireland. A north-south ministerial council was to work to facilitate cooperation between the two Irelands. The Good Friday Agreement offered a means to examine the depth of the commitment to reshape or retain the arbitrary boundaries separating Northern Ireland and the Irish Republic.

The accord was approved in twin referendums held in Northern Ireland and the Irish Republic, with Catholics overwhelmingly approving of the agreement and Protestants splitting their votes in half. This foreshadowed more divisions within Unionist ranks, while a group, referring to itself as the Real IRA, also appeared, insisting Sinn Féin not participate in the Belfast assembly. The Real IRA set off a car bomb in Omagh, County Tyrone, on August 15, 1998, a busy weekend afternoon, killing 28, half of them women, along with seven children; one more victim died shortly thereafter. In July, Unionist marchers again showed up on Garvaghy Road, leading to a firebombing of a Catholic home that resulted in the horrific deaths of three young boys. Soon, the Loyalist Volunteer Force announced it was halting operations, bringing to a close actions by Protestant paramilitaries. On September 1, Gerry Adams declared, "Violence must be a thing of the past—over, done with."[120] Nine days later, he met with David Trimble, the first such gathering between a top republican and a key figure in the Unionist camp in 76 years.

Violence continued to occur at times, but efforts to implement the Good Friday Agreement, which garnered the 1998 Nobel Peace Prize for Hume and Trimble, did as well. Cross-border bodies appeared, grappling with such issues as commercial developments. In late 1999, George Mitchell returned to Belfast,

On February 25, 2000, Sinn Féin leader Gerry Adams speaks at a press conference in West Belfast. He would become one of the most publicly recognized faces of the Irish Republican movement.

striving to break a deadlock that had arisen regarding decommission. Nevertheless, following the so-called D'Hondt rules, Sinn Féin, SDLP, Unionists, and even the Democratic Unionists of Ian Paisley occupied seats in an executive council headed by David Trimble. The post of education minister came to filled by Martin McGuinness. After less than three months, however, the executive collapsed as the question of decommissioned IRA weapons erupted still one more time. The IRA placated many, but certainly not all, by announcing that its arms would be "completely and verifiably put beyond use," and by its promise to allow international figures to examine its arms dumps.[121] By 2001, the SDLP saw John Hume resign his leadership post and Sinn Féin win more electoral spots.

Concerned that Unionists would adopt a strategy of absention, the British government shut down the National Assembly on October 14, 2002, thereby resuming direct rule, at least temporarily. The Unionists claimed that the IRA had yet to demonstrate a genuine commitment to democratic processes. New elections in late 2003 saw Paisley's DUP win the largest number of seats, followed by Sinn Féin. However, observers pointed to the fact that Peter Robinson, Paisley's more moderate deputy, shaped the DUP's election campaign, and that Sinn Féin had increasingly distanced itself from the IRA's military campaign. Still, Unionists continued to insist on the complete disbanding of the IRA, while nationalists demanded greater reform, demilitarization, and restoration of local institutions. In early 2004, critical reports came out regarding British security practices during both Bloody Sunday and other stages of the Troubles, which had taken nearly 4,000 lives. Prime Minister Tony Blair established a June deadline for the political deadlock in Northern Ireland to end and urged that paramilitary forces cease operations altogether.

In the early years of the twenty-first century, Northern nationalists and Unionists continued to clash about the arbitrary borders that shaped Northern Ireland, less frequently by resort to arms, but still often fiercely in a rhetorical fashion. While Unionists retained their allegiance to the British crown, Northern nationalists viewed the separation of the Six Northern Counties from the Irish Republic as an unfortunate, if not wholly illegitimate violation of the principle of self-determination. Certain inherently divisive issues still loomed large, including the right of Catholics to engage in self-protection, the unfair treatment accorded Northern Catholics, fears of Protestants regarding their existence in a unified Catholic state, and the question of the very legitimacy of a state established by arbitrary borders in the fashion Northern Ireland had been. The people of Britain itself appeared split regarding whether Northern Ireland should maintain its connections to the Union, with a plurality indicating support for a united Ireland. Northern Ireland remained in flux, with the old, decisive Protestant majority having dropped to barely half the population.

Such developments suggest that arbitrary borders in a landscape like Northern Ireland's will remain elusive for an indefinite period. Initially intended to ensure control by Scottish and English Protestants transplanted to Ulster, those very borders continued to divide Protestants and Catholics, Unionists and nationalists, into the early stages of the twenty-first century. On a more universalistic note, the Northern Ireland experience suggests the problems inherent in relying on arbitrary borders, which necessarily remain elusive, subject to change, and inherently controversial. Designed to resolve ethnic, religious, or ideological problems, borders that are artificially devised remain susceptible to being redrawn altogether by sectarian divisions, hardly conducive to easy solutions of a geographical or political cast.

750 BCE	Celts arrive in Ireland. Eventually, Gaelic civilization emerges.
350 CE	Christianity begins to have an impact in Ireland.
432	St. Patrick arrives in Ireland.
700	There are approximately 150 kingdoms in Ireland.
795	The Vikings conduct major invasion of Ireland.
841	The Vikings establish Ireland's first fortified settlements, including one in Dublin.
1002	Brian Boru becomes powerful high king, whose authority is widely acknowledged.

750 BCE
Celts arrive in Ireland

1649
Oliver Cromwell carries
out invasion of Ireland

1558–1603
Elizabeth I solidifies
English dominance

1845–48
Young Ireland
movement appears;
Great Famine occurs

750 BCE   1845–48

1603–1625
James I settles English
and Scottish Protestants
in northern Ireland

1169
The Normans
invade Ireland

1801
The Act of Union
movement
incorporates
Ireland

1014	Boru triumphs at the Battle of Clontarf, but is killed.
1169	The Normans invade Ireland.
1171	Henry II arrives in Ireland.
1250s	Normans achieve control over most of Ireland, but not Western Ulster.
1366	The Statutes of Kilkenny are issued.
1494	Poynings' Law is announced.
1541	Henry VIII proclaims himself King of Ireland.
1558–1603	Elizabeth I solidifies English dominance. She initiates "scorched earth policies" and the plantation program.
1595–1603	Hugh O'Neill leads a revolt in the north.

1920–21
Britain and Ireland wage war against one another

1972
Bloody Sunday occurs in Derry

1993
The Downing Street Declaration is signed

1949
The Republic of Ireland is established

1920–21   **1998**

1922–23
The Irish Civil War takes place

1969
Sectarian rioting takes place in northern Ireland

1998
The Good Friday Agreement is signed

1985
The Anglo-Irish Agreement is signed

1603–1625	James I settles English and Scottish Protestants in northern Ireland.
1607	The Flight of the Earls takes place.
1641	Uprising occurs in Ulster, in response to Charles II's autocratic rule.
1649	Oliver Cromwell carries out invasion of Ireland. Cromwell demands the relocation of property-owning Catholics, while thousands of Irish starve.
1689–1691	Having fled to Ireland, James II attempts to regain his throne. William of Orange defeats him at the Battle of the Boyne. The Treaty of Limerick promises justice for Catholics. The Catholic army departs in the Flight of the Wild Geese.
1704	The Penal Codes begin to be initiated.
1782	The all-Protestant Irish Volunteers appear; Hugh Grattan demands Irish legislative autonomy.
1780s	Sectarian warfare pitting the Protestant Peep o'Day Boys against the Catholic Defenders.
1791	Wolfe Tone establishes the United Irishmen.
1795	The Battle of the Diamond occurs, and the Orange Order is established.
1798	Following failed armed revolt, Wolfe Tone commits suicide, becoming a martyr for Irish republicanism.
1801	The Act of Union incorporates Ireland.
1823	Daniel O'Connor established the Irish Catholic Association.
1829	Following protest by newly elected MP O'Connor, the Catholic; Emancipation Act is passed.
1840s	The Young Ireland movement appears.
1845–1848	Ireland endures the Great Famine.
1850s–1860s	The Unionist Orange Order appears, along with the Irish Republican Brotherhood.
1879–1890s	Michael Davitt and Charles Steward Parnell found the Irish National League. Parnell conducts campaign for Home Rule, which is supported by Prime Minister William Gladstone, but a scandal ends Parnell's political career.

1893	The Irish Gaelic League is established.
1914	The start of World War II results in a postponement of Home Rule.
1916	The unsuccessful Easter Rising unfolds; The execution of 16 Rising leaders produces support for Irish republicanism.
1920–1921	Britain and Ireland wage war against one another.; Partition of Northern Ireland occurs, as does the creation of the Irish Free State.
1922–1923	The Irish Civil War takes place; Arthur Griffith dies and Michael Collins is assassinated.
1932	Eamon de Valera become president of the Irish Free State.
1949	The Republic of Ireland is established.
1955–1962	The IRA conducts the border wars into Northern Ireland.
1963–1969	Captain Terence O'Neill attempts reform in Northern Ireland.
1969	Sectarian rioting occurs; British troops are sent to Northern Ireland.
1971	The Provisional IRA initiates drive to force Britain out of Ulster.
1972	Bloody Sunday occurs in Derry.
1975–1981	IRA prisoners protest prison conditions, leading to hunger strikes.
1985	The Anglo-Irish Agreement is signed.
1993	The Downing Street Declaration is issued.
1998	The Good Friday Agreement is signed.

Absention: The idea that Irish members of Parliament should abstain from sitting in Westminster and instead should convene in Dublin, boycott British administration, establish their own courts, and collect taxes.

Anglo-Irish Treaty: Treaty of 1921 that established an Irish Free State, made up of 26 of Ireland's Counties.

Celtic: Used to describe the language and culture of the Celts, tribes from parts of Spain, France, and Great Britain, who arrived in Ireland between the sixth and fourth centuries B.C.E.

CS gas: A non-lethal riot control agent, commonly called tear gas.

Dail Eireann: The Irish parliament.

Direct rule: Conducting the administration of Northern Ireland directly from Westminster, this was the official British policy from March 1972 until the establishment of the Northern Ireland Assembly under the terms of the Good Friday Agreement in 1998.

Eire: The Gaelic name of the Irish Free State.

Fianna Fail: The largest political party in the Republic of Ireland, it was founded on March 23, 1926, by Eamon de Valera; it began as an anti-Treaty party.

Feudalism: A European legal and administrative system founded on the exchange of reciprocal undertakings of protection and loyalty.

Flight of the Earls: The departure of Tyrone's Hugh O'Neill and Tyrconnel's Rory O'Donnell in the early seventeenth century, which enabled the English government to take control of six of Ulster's Nine Counties.

Gaelic: The language and customs of the Celtic people; also a term for the Irish language.

Gerrymandering: the redrawing of electoral boundaries to benefit Unionists in Northern Ireland.

Ghetto: A section of a city occupied by a minority group that lives there because of social, economic, or legal pressure.

Good Friday Agreement: Signed on April 10, 1998 by the British and Irish Governments and subsequently endorsed by the voters of Northern Ireland and the Republic of Ireland; a main provision that constitutional future of Northern Ireland be determined by the democratically expressed wish of its people.

Home Rule: Refers to the movement demanding greater autonomy for Ireland, including the creation of a subsidiary Irish parliament, within the British Commonwealth.

Internment: Practice allowing the imprisonment of suspects without trial initiated by the British soldiers in Operation Demetrius in 1971.

Irish Republican Army (IRA): The army of the Irish Republic formed during the War of Independence in 1919; title claimed by several paramilitary groups, which advocate a unitary Irish state with no ties to the United Kingdom.

Irish War of Independence: The name for the campaign mounted against the Royal Irish Constabulary, the British Army, and the Black and Tans in Ireland by the Irish Republican Army.

Loyalists: Those who favor Northern Ireland remaining part of the United Kingdom and are predominantly Protestant by religion; originally used to describe those who insisted that all of Ireland remain in the United Kingdom.

Nationalists: Those who advocate the independence of Ireland from Great Britain and are predominantly Catholic by religion; originally denoted those satisfied with the Home Rule arrangement that arose from the Irish Civil War of the early 1920s; see also Republicans.

Normans: Peoples from the northern region of France, particularly those who invaded England.

Official IRA: One of the two elements of the Irish Republican Army (the other being the Provisional IRA) that emerged from the ideological split in 1969.

Official Sinn Féin: Split along with the Official IRA from the Provisional Sinn Féin/ Provisional IRA at the end of 1969; over time, the Official Sinn Féin faded away.

Pale: The fortified arbitrary border around Dublin that was historically controlled by English officials.

Parochial schools: Educational institutions run by the church.

Plantations: Refers to the settlement of English and Scottish Protestants in northern Ireland in the seventeenth century.

Primogeniture: Practice that enabled first-born children (usually sons) to inherit all property rights and titles.

Provisional IRA: A militant splinter group of the Official IRA that formed in the late 1960s and used terrorism and guerilla warfare with the goal of ending British rule in Northern Ireland and achieving a united independent Ireland; generally referred to as the IRA.

Provisional Sinn Féin: Became the political voice of the northern nationalists who saw IRA attacks as the means of forcing an end to British rule; currently the strongest nationalist party in Northern Ireland.

Republicans: Those who advocate the complete independence of Ireland from Great Britain and are predominantly Catholic by religion.

Royal Ulster Constabulary (RUC): Founded out of the Royal Irish Constabulary, the RUC was the police force in Northern Ireland from 1922 to 2001.

Sinn Féin: An Irish political party founded almost 100 years ago by Arthur Griffith that evolved into a number of organizations carrying the name.

Special Category Status: Under special category status, political prisoners were housed in separate wings, allowed to wear their own clothes, and receive more visits.

Special Powers Act of 1922: Act that enabled security forces in the North to search homes without warrants, prevent meetings and rallies from being held, employ violence during interrogations of suspects, and carry out hangings.

Stormont: A district outside of Belmont and site of Northern Ireland's government.

Taoiseach: The prime minister of the Republic of Ireland.

The Troubles: The period of violence in Northern Ireland beginning with the civil rights marches in the late 1960s to the political resolution enshrined in the 1998 Good Friday Agreement.

Ulster: One of the historic provinces of the island of Ireland, consisting of nine counties: three of these are part of the Republic of Ireland; the remaining six counties are known as Northern Ireland.

Unionists: Those who favor Northern Ireland remaining part of the United Kingdom and are predominantly Protestant by religion.

Westminster: The Palace of Westminster, which houses the Parliament of the United Kingdom.

Chapter 1

1. Quoted in Marc Mulholland, *The Longest War: Northern Ireland's Troubled History.* New York: Oxford University Press, 2002, p. 55.
2. Quoted in Peter Pringle and Philip Jacobson, *Those Are Real Bullets: Bloody Sunday, Derry, 1972.* New York: Grove Press, 2001, p. 29.
3. Quoted in Mulholland, *The Longest War,* 54.
4. Quoted in Pringle, *Those Are Real Bullets,* 33.
5. Quoted in Jack Holland, *Hope against History: The Course of Conflict in Northern Ireland.* New York: Henry Holt and Company, 1999, p. 15.
6. Quoted in David McKittrick and David McVea, *Making Sense of the Troubles: The Story of the Conflict in Northern Ireland.* Chicago: New Amsterdam Books, 2002, p. 47.
7. Quoted in Holland, *Hope against History,* 15.
8. Ibid.
9. Quoted in Michael Farrell, *Northern Ireland: The Orange State.* London: Pluto Press, 1976, p. 251.
10. Quoted in Brian Feeney, *Sinn Féin: A Hundred Turbulent Years.* Madison, Wisconsin: The University of Wisconsin Press, 2003, p. 255.
11. Quoted in Terry Golway, *For the Cause of Liberty: A Thousand Years of Ireland's Heroes.* New York: Simon & Schuster, 2000, p. 295.
12. Quoted in Pringle, *Those Are Real Bullets,* 35.
13. Quoted in Feeney, *Sinn Féin,* 261.
14. Quoted in Pringle, *Those Are Real Bullets,* 34.
15. Quoted in Farrell, *Northern Ireland,* 281.
16. Quoted in Pringle, *Those Are Real Bullets,* 47, 56.
17. Ibid., 75.
18. Quoted in Golway, *For the Cause of Liberty,* 298.
19. Quoted in J. Bowyer Bell, *The Irish Troubles: A Generation of Violence 1967–1992.* New York: St. Martin's Press, 1993, p. 272.

Chapter 2

20. Quoted in J.H. Andrews, "A Geographer's View of Irish History," in *The Course of Irish History,* ed. T. W. Moody and F. X. Martin (Lanham, Maryland: Robert Rinehard Publishers, 2001), p. 10.
21. Quoted in David Willis McCullough, ed., *Wars of the Irish Kings: A Thousand Years of Struggle from the Age of Myth through the Reign of Queen Elizabeth I.* New York: Crown Publishers, 2000, p. 105.
22. Quoted in Marcus Tanner. *Ireland's Holy Wars: The Struggle for a Nation's Soul 1500–2000.* New Haven: Yale University Press, 2001, p. 40.
23. Ibid., 40.
24. Ibid., 99–100.
25. Ibid., 121.
26. Ibid., 135.
27. Quoted in Charles Duff, *Six Days to Shake an Empire.* South Brunswick: A.S. Barnes and Co., Inc., 1966, p. 54.
28. Quoted in John Darby, ed., *Northern Ireland: The Background to the Conflict.* Syracuse: Appletree Press, 1983, p. 16.
29. Quoted in Neil Longley York, *Neither Kingdom nor Nation: The Irish Quest for Constitutional Rights, 1698–1800.* Washington, D.C.: The Catholic University of America Press, 1994, pp. 134–135.
30. Quoted in Thomas Bartlett. *The Fall and Rise of the Irish Nation: The Catholic Question 1690–1830.* Savage, Maryland: Barnes & Noble Books, 1992, p. 126.
31. Quoted in Breandan O hEithir, *A Pocket History of Ireland.* Dublin: The O'Brien Press, 2001, p. 37.
32. Ibid.
33. Quoted in Feeney, *Sinn Féin,* 20–21.
34. Quoted in James H. Murphy, *Abject Loyalty: Nationalism and Monarchy in Ireland during the Reign of Queen Victoria.* Cork: Cork University Press, 2001, p. 148.
35. Quoted in T. W. Moody, "Fenianism, Home Rule and the Land War 1850–91," in *The Course of Irish History,* p. 342.

Chapter 3

36. Quoted in Feeney, *Sinn Féin,* 80.
37. Quoted in Mulholland, *The Longest War,* 23.

38. Quoted in Duff, *Six Days to Shake an Empire*, 73.
39. Quoted in Thomas Hennessey, *A History of Northern Ireland*. New York: St. Martin's Press, 1999, p. 3.
40. Quoted in Mulholland, *The Longest War*, 24.
41. Quoted in Thomas M. Coffey, *Agony at Easter: The 1916 Uprising*. Toronto: The MacMillan Company, 1969, p. 14.
42. O hEithir, *A Pocket History of Ireland*, 56.
43. Quoted in Tim Patrick Coogan, *The IRA*. New York: Palgrave, 2000, p. 20.
44. Quoted in Max Caulfield, *The Easter Rebellion*. New York: Holt, Rinehart and Winston, 1963, pp. 305–306.
45. Quoted in Coffey, *Agony at Easter*, 252.
46. Quoted in Leon O Broin, *Dublin Castle & the 1916 Uprising*. New York: New York University Press, 1971, p. 166.
47. Quoted in O hEithir, *A Pocket History of Ireland*, 57.
48. Quoted in Coffey, *Agony at Easter*, 262.
49. Quoted in Duff, *Six Days to Shake an Empire*, 211.
50. Quoted in W. B. Yeats, "Easter 1916."
51. Quoted in Duff, *Six Days to Shake an Empire*, 199.

Chapter 4

52. Quoted in Tanner, *Ireland's Holy Wars*, 283.
53. Quoted in Duff, *Six Days to Shake an Empire*, 232.
54. Ibid., 236.
55. Quoted in Feeney, *Sinn Féin*, 115.
56. "Irish Declaration of Independence," January 21, 1919.
57. Quoted in Hennessey, *A History of Northern Ireland*, pp. 8–9.
58. Ibid., p. 6.
59. Quoted in Coogan, *The IRA*, 26.
60. Quoted in Feeney, *Sinn Féin*, 147.

Chapter 5

61. Quoted in Coogan, *The IRA*, 27.
62. Quoted in Hennessey, *A History of Northern Ireland*, 22–23.
63. Quoted in Richard English, *Armed Struggle: The History of the IRA*. New York: Oxford University Press, 2003, p. 31.
64. Quoted in Farrell, *Northern Ireland*, 73.
65. Quoted in Feeney, *Sinn Féin*, 135.

66. Ibid., 154.
67. Quoted in English, *Armed Struggle*, 36.

Chapter 6

68. Ibid., 40.
69. Ibid., 42.
70. Quoted in Farrell, *Northern Ireland*, 127.
71. Ibid., 130.
72. Quoted in Hennessey, *A History of Northern Ireland*, 67.
73. *The Irish Free State Constitution.*
74. Quoted in English, *Armed Struggle*, 60.
75. Quoted in Coogan, *The IRA*, 125.
76. Quoted in Hennessey, *A History of Northern Ireland*, 92.
77. Quoted in Patrick Buckland, *A History of Northern Ireland*. New York: Holmes & Meier Publishers, Inc., 1981, p. 85.

Chapter 7

78. Quoted in Farrell, *Northern Ireland*, 192.
79. Quoted in Coogan, *The IRA*, 256, 264.
80. Quoted in English, *Armed Struggle*, 73.
81. Quoted in Coogan, *The IRA*, 329.
82. Quoted in Buckland, *A History of Northern Ireland*, 105.
83. Quoted in Henry Patterson, *Ireland Since 1939*. New York: Oxford University Press, 2002, p. 157.
84. Quoted in Farrell, *Northern Ireland*, 221–222.
85. Quoted in Bell, *The Irish Troubles*, 28.
86. Ibid., 38.
87. Ibid., 39.

Chapter 8

88. Quoted in Mulholland, *The Longest War*, 60.
89. Quoted in Patterson, *Ireland Since 1939*, 161.
90. Quoted in Coogan, *The Troubles: Ireland's Ordeal 1966–1996 and the Search for Peace*. New York: Palgrave, 2002, p. 53.
91. Quoted in Farrell, *Northern Ireland*, 236.
92. Quoted in Tanner, *Ireland's Holy Wars*, 362, 364.
93. Quoted in Farrell, *Northern Ireland*, 256.
94. Quoted in Coogan, *The Troubles*, 94.

Chapter 9

95. Quoted in Holland, *Hope against History*, 26.
96. Quoted in Bell, *The Irish Troubles*, 122.
97. Ibid., 145.
98. Quoted in Hennessey, *A History of Northern Ireland*, 173.
99. Ibid., 181.
100. Quoted in English, *Armed Struggle*, 144.
101. Quoted in Coogan, *The Troubles*, 161.
102. Quoted in McKittrick, *Making Sense of the Troubles*, 80.
103. Quoted in Holland, *Hope against History*, 60.
104. Quoted in Bell, *The Irish Troubles*, 393.
105. Quoted in Holland, *Hope against History*, 83.
106. Quoted in Coogan, *The IRA*, 547.
107. Quoted in McKittrick, *Making Sense of the Troubles*, 139–140.
108. Quoted in Hennessey, *A History of Northern Ireland*, 261.

Chapter 10

109. Quoted in English, *Armed Struggle*, 244.
110. Quoted in McKittrick, *Making Sense of the Troubles*, 160.
111. Ibid., 165.
112. "Anglo–Irish Agreement 1985."
113. Quoted in Feeney, *Sinn Féin*, 349, 357.
114. Quoted in English, *Armed Struggle*, 269–270.
115. "Joint Declaration on Peace: The Downing Street Declaration," December 15, 1993.
116. Ibid., 271–272.
117. Quoted in Coogan, *The Troubles*, 449, 451, 452. (changed from Cooney)
118. Quoted in Hennessey, *A History of Northern Ireland*, 300.
119. Quoted in McKittrick, *Making Sense of the Troubles*, 211.
120. Quoted in Holland, *Hope against History*, 223.
121. Quoted in McKittrick, *Making Sense of the Troubles*, 228.

Andrews, J.H. "A Geographer's View of Irish History." In T.W. Moody and F.X. Martin, eds. *The Course of Irish History*. 4th ed. Lanham, MD: Robert Rinehart Publishers, 2001.

Bartlett, Thomas. *The Fall and Rise of the Irish Nation: The Catholic Question 1690–1830*. Savage, MD: Rowman & Littlefield, 1992.

Bell, J. Bowyer. *The Irish Troubles: A Generation of Violence 1967–1992*. New York: St. Martin's Press, 1993.

Buckland, Patrick. *A History of Northern Ireland*. New York: Holmes & Meier Publishers, Inc., 1981.

Caulfield, Max. *The Easter Rebellion*. New York: Holt, Rinehart and Winston, 1963.

Coffey, Thomas M. *Agony at Easter: The 1916 Irish Uprising*. Toronto: The MacMillan Company, 1969.

Coogan, Tim Patrick. *The IRA*. New York: Palgrave, 2000.

_____. *The Troubles: Ireland's Ordeal 1966–1996 and the Search for Peace*. New York: Palgrave, 2002.

Darby, John, ed. *Northern Ireland: The Background to the Conflict*. Syracuse, NY: Appletree Press, 1983.

Duff, Charles. *Six Days to Shake an Empire*. South Brunswick, NJ: A.S. Barnes and Co., Inc., 1966.

English, Richard. *Armed Struggle: The History of the IRA*. New York: Oxford University Press, 2003.

Farrell, Michael. *Northern Ireland: The Orange State*. London: Pluto Press, 1976.

Feeney, Brian. *Sinn Féin: A Hundred Turbulent Years*. Madison, WI: The University of Wisconsin Press, 2003.

Fraser, T.G. *Partition in Ireland, India and Palestine: Theory and Practice*. New York: St. Martin's Press, 1984.

Golway, Terry. *For the Cause of Liberty: A Thousand Years of Ireland's Heroes.* New York: Simon & Schuster, 2000.

Hennessey, Thomas. *A History of Northern Ireland.* New York: St. Martin's Press, 1999.

Holland, Jack. *Hope against History: The Course of Conflict in Northern Ireland.* New York: Henry Holt and Company, 1999.

Keogh, Dermot. *Twentieth-Century Ireland: Nation and State.* New York: St. Martin's Press, 1994.

McCullough, David Willis, ed. *Wars of the Irish Kings: A Thousand Years of Struggle from the Age of Myth through the Reign of Queen Elizabeth I.* New York: Crown Publishers, 2000.

McKittrick, David and David McVea. *Making Sense of the Troubles: The Story of the Conflict in Northern Ireland.* Chicago: New Amsterdam Books, 2002.

Moody, T.W. "Fenianism, Home Rule and the Land War 1850–91." In T.W. Moody and F.X. Martin, eds. *The Course of Irish History.* 4th ed. Lanham, MD: Robert Rinehart Publishers, 2001.

Moody, T.W. and F.X. Martin, eds. *The Course of Irish History.* 4th ed. Lanham, MD: Robert Rinehart Publishers, 2001.

Mulholland, Marc. *The Longest War: Northern Ireland's Troubled History.* Oxford: Oxford University Press, 2002.

Mullan, Don. *Eyewitness Bloody Sunday: The Truth.* Dublin: Merlin Publishing, 2002.

Murphy, James H. *Abject Loyalty: Nationalism and Monarchy in Ireland during the Reign of Queen Victoria.* Cork: Cork University Press, 2001.

O Broin, Leon. *Dublin Castle & the 1916 Uprising.* New York: New York University Press, 1971.

O hEithir, Breandan. *A Pocket History of Ireland.* Dublin: The O'Brien Press, 2001.

Patterson, Henry. *Ireland Since 1939.* New York: Oxford University Press, 2002.

Pereval-Maxwell, M. *The Outbreak of the Irish Rebellion of 1641.* Montreal: McGill-Queen's University Press, 1994.

Pringle, Peter and Philip Jacobson. *Those Are Real Bullets: Bloody Sunday, Derry, 1972.* New York: Grove Press, 2000.

Shaw, Antony, compiler. *Portable Ireland: A Visual Reference to All Things Irish.* Philadelphia: Running Press, 2002.

Tanner, Marcus. *Ireland's Holy Wars: The Struggle for a Nation's Soul 1500–2000.* New Haven: Yale University Press, 2001.

York, Neil Longley. *Neither Kingdom nor Nation: The Irish Quest for Constitutional Rights, 1698–1800.* Washington, D.C.: The Catholic University of America Press, 1994.

Bew, Paul, Peter Gibbon, and Henry Patterson. *The State in Northern Ireland 1921–72: Political Forces and Social Classes.* New York: St. Martin's Press, 1979.

Bruce, Steve. *The Red Hand: Protestant Paramilitaries in Northern Ireland.* New York: Oxford University Press, 1992.

Dillon, Martin. *The Dirty War: Covert Strategies and Tactics Used in Political Conflicts.* New York: Routledge, 1990.

English, Richard, and Graham Walker, eds. *Unionism in Modern Ireland: New Perspectives on Politics and Culture.* New York: St. Martin Press, Inc., 1996.

Farrell, Sean. *Rituals and Riots: Sectarian Violence and Political Culture in Ulster,* Lexington, KY: The University Press of Kentucky, 2000.

Harnden, Toby. *'Bandit Country': The IRA and South Armagh.* London: Coronet Books, 2000.

Howe, Stephen. *Ireland and Empire: Colonial Legacies in Irish History and Culture.* New York: Oxford University Press, 2000.

Loughlin, James. *Gladstone, Home Rule and the Ulster Question 1882–93.* Atlantic Highlands, NJ: Humanities Press International, Inc., 1987.

Martin, F.X., ed. *Leaders and Men of the Easter Rising: Dublin 1916.* New York: Cornell University Press, 1967.

O'Leary, Brendan, and John McGarry. *The Politics of Antagonism: Understanding Northern Ireland.* London: The Athlone Press, 1993.

Rose, Peter. *How the Troubles Came to Northern Ireland.* New York: St. Martin's Press, Inc., 2000.

Wright, Frank. *Two Lands on One Soil: Ulster Politics before Home Rule.* New York: St. Martin's Press, 1996.

page:

Frontis: 21st Century Publishing
3:   AFP/NMI
35: AP/World Wide Photos
43: © Hulton-Deutsch Collection/CORBIS
45: © Hulton-Deutsch Collection/CORBIS
46: Hulton Getty Photo Archive/NMI

52: AP/World Wide Photos
54: © Hulton-Deutsch Collection/CORBIS
65: Hulton Getty Photo Archive/NMI
88: © Bettman/CORBIS
99: Zuma Press/NMI
113: AP/World Wide Photos

Robert C. Cottrell Professor of History and American Studies at California State University, Chico, is the author of many books, including *Izzy: A Biography of I.F. Stone, Roger Nash Baldwin and the American Civil Liberties Union, The Best Pitcher in Baseball: The Life of Rube Foster, Negro League Giant,* and *Uncertain Order: The World in the Twentieth Century.* Named the Outstanding Professor at CSUC in 1998, Professor Cottrell received the 2000 Wang Family Excellence Award for Social & Behavioral Sciences & Public Services, a system-wide honor for the 23 campuses that make up the California State University. *Northern Ireland and England: The Troubles* is his third book for Chelsea House.

George J. Mitchell served as chairman of the peace negotiations in Northern Ireland during the 1990s. Under his leadership, an historic accord, ending decades of conflict, was agreed to by the governments of Ireland and the United Kingdom and the political parties in Northern Ireland. In May 1998, the agreement was overwhelmingly endorsed by a referendum of the voters of Ireland, North and South. Senator Mitchell's leadership earned him worldwide praise and a Nobel Peace Prize nomination. He accepted his appointment to the U.S. Senate in 1980. After leaving the Senate, Senator Mitchell joined the Washington, D.C. law firm of Piper Rudnick, where he now practices law. Senator Mitchell's life and career have embodied a deep commitment to public service and he continues to be active in worldwide peace and disarmament efforts.

James I. Matray is professor of history and chair at California State University, Chico. He has published more than forty articles and book chapters on U.S.-Korean relations during and after World War II. Author of *The Reluctant Crusade: American Foreign Policy in Korea, 1941–1950 and Japan's Emergence as a Global Power,* his most recent publication is *East Asia and the United States: An Encyclopledia of Relations Since 1784.* Matray also is international columnist for the *Donga libo* in South Korea.